WEST SIDE STORY

THE JETS, THE SHARKS, AND THE MAKING OF A CLASSIC

TURNER **CLASSIC** MOVIES

WEST SIDE STORY

THE JETS, THE SHARKS, AND THE MAKING OF A CLASSIC

RICHARD BARRIOS

Running Press
PHILADELPHIA

Running Press
Hachette Book Group
1290 Avenue of the Americas, New York, NY 10104
www.runningpress.com
@Running_Press

Printed in China

First Edition: May 2020

Published by Running Press, an imprint of Perseus Books, LLC, a subsidiary of Hachette Book Group, Inc. The Running Press name and logo is a trademark of the Hachette Book Group.

The Hachette Speakers Bureau provides a wide range of authors for speaking events. To find out more, go to www.hachettespeakersbureau.com or call (866) 376-6591.

The publisher is not responsible for websites (or their content) that are not owned by the publisher.

Image Credits: Pages 9, 10, 13, 14, 16 (both), 19, 22-23, 25, 35, 36 (bottom), 39, 41 (top), 51, 54-55, 56, 65, 75, 100, 118 (top), 140-41, 146, 150 (top), 162-63, 164, 167, 178, 190, 193: Courtesy Photofest. Pages 28, 33, 43, 66, 79 (top), 80-81, 88 (top), 92, 94, 95, 97, 102, 105 (middle), 110-11, 116, 118-19, 125, 126-27, 128, 130, 134, 135, 137, 150 (bottom), 155 (top): Courtesy Manoah Bowman. All other photography courtesy Turner Classic Movies, Inc.

Print book cover and interior design by Celeste Joyce.

Library of Congress Control Number: 2019953642

ISBNs: 978-0-7624-6948-2 (hardcover), 978-0-7624-6946-8 (ebook)

1010

10 9 8 7 6 5 4 3 2 1

THE SCREEN ACHIEVES ONE OF THE GREAT ENTERTAINMENTS

IN THE HISTORY OF MOTION PICTURES

MIRISCH PICTURES PRESENTS

"WEST SIDE STORY"

A ROBERT WISE PRODUCTION

STARRING NATALIE WOOD

RICHARD BEYMER   RUSS TAMBLYN
RITA MORENO   GEORGE CHAKIRIS

DIRECTED BY ROBERT WISE AND JEROME ROBBINS SCREENPLAY BY ERNEST LEHMAN

ASSOCIATE PRODUCER SAUL CHAPLIN   CHOREOGRAPHY BY JEROME ROBBINS
MUSIC BY LEONARD BERNSTEIN LYRICS BY STEPHEN SONDHEIM
BASED UPON THE STAGE PLAY PRODUCED BY ROBERT E. GRIFFITH AND HAROLD S. PRINCE

BOOK BY ARTHUR LAURENTS

PLAY CONCEIVED, DIRECTED AND CHOREOGRAPHED BY JEROME ROBBINS
PRODUCTION DESIGNED BY BORIS LEVEN · FILMED IN PANAVISION® 70 · TECHNICOLOR®
PRESENTED BY MIRISCH PICTURES, INC   IN ASSOCIATION WITH SEVEN ARTS PRODUCTIONS, INC.
RELEASED THRU UNITED ARTISTS

To Spencer and Keith—
my brothers.

CONTENTS

COULD BE . . .

ABOVE: Finger snaps: Russ Tamblyn, Tucker Smith, and Tony Mordente at the beginning of the Prologue.

PAGE X: If one image can evoke an entire film, this may be the one. Jay Norman, George Chakiris, and Eddie Verso, on the 200 block of West 68th Street in Manhattan.

ALL IT TAKES IS THOSE FINGER snaps. As soon as we hear them, we're there, we're committed, we're riveted. Even before the gang members begin to dance, before Maria and Tony meet, before "Tonight" or "America" or "I Feel Pretty," we've been drawn in. It's always that way with *West Side Story*. From its premiere in 1961 up to now, it has moved beyond ordinary limits of cinema. It has become lodged in our memories and hearts and after six decades, with stage productions, endless homages and parodies, and even with a remake, it continues to hypnotize audiences in a way few works do. Its excitement, its music, romance, and tragedy—even the parts so raw that they can be difficult to watch—none of it can be compared with any other film. Shockingly enough, it's perhaps more relevant now than when it was new, with conflicts still being played out in the world in many painful ways. Few movies are anywhere as overwhelming as this one, especially when it is seen on a massive screen, as its creators intended. For those creators, the complications of making it were, on a steady basis, all but unimaginable. Fortunately, the rewards of their hard work are all remarkably apparent. From the breathless and bracing overture all the way to the stunningly imaginative credits at the end, the momentum never lets up. Corny? Not a chance. As one of its characters sings, it's "cool," everlastingly so. And, with its dance, music, and use of Manhattan locations, also hot.

Unlike nearly every movie made from a musical show, *West Side Story* is unique: in spite of its high-profile source, it has thrived on its own. Where a *South Pacific* (1958) or a *My Fair Lady* (1964) will eternally be "the film of the show," *West Side Story* stands on its inherent merit and impact as well as that of its material. It is because of that impact that the songs became standards, and that the show's subsequent popularity has remained so constant. It's due to the film, really, that so much of *West Side Story* lives permanently in our minds: the sight of tough guys dancing down the street, the use of fire escapes to evoke romantic longing, the depiction of time literally standing still when two lovers meet for the first time, the notion that two battling street gangs can assume the dimensions of classical tragedy.

In the theater, *West Side Story* had been completely without precedent, breaking new ground in subject matter, unity of music and dance, overall presentation, and seriousness of intent. Leonard Bernstein's music, alternately lyrical and jagged, was uniquely coupled with Stephen Sondheim's bright lyrics and the *Romeo and Juliet*–inspired plot, with its Us-versus-Them ethnic clash that was both pertinent and prophetic. The script, by Arthur Laurents, was lean and powerful. Most of all, there was Jerome Robbins, whose choreography and direction, whose sheer vision, were of a caliber not previously seen. The result was electrifying, yet so theatrical that

it could not be put on the screen verbatim. It was left to the movie's producer and codirector, Robert Wise, to grasp that a film version would need to stake out entirely new ground. It could not be a copy of the show, nor could it be like anything else that came before. And it wasn't.

As a film, *West Side Story* accomplished monumental feats. It ran literally for years, so pervasive and inescapable that, at the time, it was next to impossible to go to a store and not see the soundtrack album (on LP, of course) or the paperback novelization, reprinted nearly in perpetuity. Both the soundtrack and the book sported that distinctive, indelible logo with the fire escape and red background that evoke the film so effortlessly. Its influence goes well beyond that of a conventional film hit, past even the generations of young people it has inspired to become dancers or become involved in musical theater. Its unflinching portrayal of prejudice and hostility has heightened an awareness of cultural inequities and societal conflicts and, in doing so, has delivered messages of brother- and sisterhood, peace, and healing. In the realm of popular entertainment, such achievements and messages are incredibly rare. In a much lighter vein, and not surprising with a work this pervasive, it has inspired jokes and homages so numerous they are impossible to count. Even animated TV series such as *Family Guy* and *Animaniacs* have gotten in on the act. (The latter show was executive-produced by Steven Spielberg.) Yet it's the original that stays eternal and even fresh. Like that legendary one-woman tribute Cher paid to it when she played all the lead roles in a 1978 television special, *West Side Story* remains a stand-alone accomplishment, glorious and irreplaceable.

Being a movie musical, *West Side Story* falls into the grand procession of influential works that begins in 1929 with that creaky pioneer *The Broadway Melody,* continues through *42nd Street* (1933) and the Astaire-Rogers films in the 1930s, and moves on to *The Wizard of Oz* (1939), *Meet Me in St. Louis* (1944), *Singin' in the Rain* (1952), and others, later to *The Sound of Music* (1965), *Cabaret* (1972), and all the way up to *La La Land* (2016). It equals these in significance, but it could not be more different in tone and overall direction. It's not that *West Side Story* is so much better than, say, *Top Hat* (1935) or *Singin' in the Rain*, because in the estimations of many it's not. What it is, incontestably, is *different:* in its goals and ambitions, its methods and intentions, its effects and impressions. This is made clear in the very first minutes, with that bravura overture playing over abstract designs that finally dissolve into a Manhattan skyline. This is obviously a film that sees itself as a major work. Neither pompous nor self-satisfied, yet always aware that it is striving for quality and meaning outside and beyond conventional boundaries of musical theater or film.

"Epic" and "musical" are two words generally not found in each other's company, but what is *West Side Story* if not a musical epic? In its themes and presentation, it takes a big approach, not unlike other blockbuster movies of its time like *Spartacus* (1960) and *Lawrence of Arabia* (1962). While it doesn't slight the details, it is definitely a film that sets out to be big in scale, attitude, and intent. While most find this monumentality to be effective, others (including film critic Pauline Kael) have found it off-putting. Movie musicals do traditionally divide audiences, and *West Side Story* is no exception. Yet, as one of the most loved of all musicals, it came by its stature honestly and, as a look at its creation makes clear, through all-but-unearthly amounts of rigor and effort.

Mentioning *West Side Story* to people elicits the dawn of excitement in people's faces. First in their eyes, then in their expression and in the finger snaps that sometimes follow. It goes further than simple recollection or nostalgia. The plain truth is that *West Side Story* has affected many people very deeply. Is it because of its neo–*Romeo and Juliet* romantic tragedy? That surely plays a role. So do the songs and those extraordinary dances full of verve, precision, and keen characterization. So, too, does Natalie Wood's star charisma, Rita Moreno's blazing conviction, Russ Tamblyn's nervy athleticism, George Chakiris's suave and vaguely sinister grace, and, for many, Richard Beymer's first-love sincerity. Those dancers, too—those men and women of great ability working hard, totally into what they're doing and completely intent on giving their best to Robbins, the camera, and the audience. All these factors matter intensely, as do the widely divergent gifts brought to the work by Wise and Robbins, and by all the artists and technicians working with them. On a production of this complexity, everyone's contribution counts for a great deal.

Traditionally and understandably, much of the credit for the film's success has gone to Robbins. To connect the dance and song with the subject matter took skill so nuanced and complex as to be almost inconceivable, and it is not uncommon, among those who worked with Robbins, to hear him referred to as a genius. His vision, which had made the show so compelling, was essential to the film, although—as will be recounted here—Hollywood and New York are far different places. One of the bottom-line verities of musical films is that they must work immensely hard to make the final result seem

effortless and organic. Robbins was a perfectionist of the first order, which made for brilliant results while causing numerous delays and budget increases. As a result, one major theme in this saga concerns the eternal struggle between art and commerce. Think of it as a sort of behind-the-scenes version of the war between the Jets and the Sharks, playing out both on the streets of New York City and on Hollywood soundstages. The positive results of this conflict were plainly evident in the final product; those that were more negative were off the screen and, often, deeply felt. Both were responsible for the way *West Side Story* turned out.

Robbins's codirector, Robert Wise, has seldom received anything like the recognition given to Robbins. Yet, in crucial ways, he had the greater responsibility and as sig-

BELOW: Richard Beymer and Natalie Wood

ABOVE: **George Chakiris as Bernardo**

nificant an impact. As producer, his was the final word in selecting the cast and crew, for all the preparatory work not concerned with dance, and for the demanding job of assembling and polishing the final product. If often a quiet presence on the set—especially by comparison with the volcanic Robbins—he offered the most competent leadership imaginable, inspiring devotion from the crew and keeping an unwieldy project moving along as steadily as humanly possible. He was as necessary to *West Side Story* as Robbins, and surely the film turned out as successfully as it did in large part because it was directed by two men who were, in so many ways, polar opposites.

If Wise and Robbins were not always in accord, they were both aware that this was a wholly unconventional production, all the more so for its being made independently outside the confines of the major movie studios that still existed. With the intensive amount of preparation required, and the enormous amount of time involved, it was one of the most costly films shot in America up to that time. In all of it—conception, planning, casting, rehearsal, shooting—nothing came easily, nothing was taken for granted, nothing took less time, effort, or money than originally anticipated, and crisis often seemed to be a daily occurrence. When the triumph of acclaim and Oscars came, each person involved would have her or his own takeaways, and not always the expected or happy ones. Since then, there has been a legacy of glory and ongoing regard and, in later years, some controversy. All of this will continue even as, in 2020, the Steven Spielberg remake looms as both tribute and competition.

With a film this famous, this celebrated, loved, and complicated, there are many stories to tell in addition to the one about Tony and Maria and the Jets and the Sharks. There is first that of the work itself and, not surprisingly, much of the *West Side Story* literature tends to concentrate on the show. Generally, the movie is brought in as something of an inevitable afterthought. This does a disservice to both history and to the movie's triumphs, so let it be stated again, as clearly and directly as that gang whistle at the beginning: the achievement and repercussions of this film are completely without parallel. It's no overstatement to note that it forever changed the way people looked at musicals and at movies in general. The wonder is that many millions still find it every bit as thrilling as they always did, and the many who have come to it later on are usually startled to find out just how much it lives up to all the hype. Where else could there be found this blending of rough realism and delicate romance, of stark immediacy and timelessness, of cutting-edge theater and big-time cinema, of anger and comity, of anguish and exhilaration, of Shakespeare and today's headlines? None of this, as will be recounted here, was achieved without great effort, nor without great talent.

The overture is now ending, and the title is coming up on the screen. It's time for *West Side Story.*

BELOW: The exhilaration of "America": Maria Jimenez, Joanne Miya (hidden), Rita Moreno, Yvonne Othon, Suzie Kaye

CHAPTER ONE

NOW IT BEGINS: FROM SHAKESPEARE TO BROADWAY

—

Six Jailed in Fight Death

San Bernardino, Aug. 21: Six youths were
jailed for investigation of murder here today in
the street fight death of Robert C. Garcia,
20, at a Saturday night teenage dance.

LOS ANGELES TIMES
August 22, 1955

ABOVE: The creative team for the original Broadway production: Stephen Sondheim, Arthur Laurents, Harold Prince, Robert Griffith, Leonard Bernstein, and Jerome Robbins

PAGE 9: First meeting: Carol Lawrence as Maria and Larry Kert as Tony

ALL IT *"FAR WEST SIDE STORY,"* perhaps, because in one sense it did not begin in New York. While the August 21 San Bernardino incident is most often cited as the motivating factor, other sources mention a *Los Angeles Times* article about gang violence on Olvera Street. What does remain reasonably certain is that composer Leonard Bernstein and writer Arthur Laurents were both in Los Angeles in August of 1955 and saw one or more articles in the *Times* about local gang violence. This helped spur them to revive a dormant project that they had begun to conceive nearly seven years earlier alongside Jerome Robbins.

Since Robbins is the single most essential person in the entire saga of *West Side Story,* it's fitting that, evidently, he was responsible for the idea in the first place. While the details are again a bit fuzzy, it appears that Robbins originated the idea of a musical updating of *Romeo and Juliet* in 1948, after discussing the play with his lover at the time, Montgomery Clift. Puzzling over the passive aspects of the character of Romeo, Clift asked Robbins if there might be any way to make the role more vital. Robbins replied by noting that the universality of Shakespeare's drama means that it can often be more comprehensible when viewed in modern terms. The feuding Montagues and Capulets, for example, could have an equivalent in something as timely as the ongoing conflict between Jews and

Catholics living on the East Side of Manhattan. Having made that comparison, Robbins began to think about Cole Porter's current Broadway hit, *Kiss Me, Kate*. It cleverly set *The Taming of the Shrew* within a modern plot, an act which did not seem to diminish or demean Shakespeare in the least. So, if it worked for Petruchio and Katharina, why not Romeo and Juliet? Robbins continued to think about it some more and then, early in 1949, contacted his friends Laurents and Bernstein. Their brainstorming took fire so quickly that within weeks it rated an article in the *New York Times*.

"Romeo" to Receive Musical Styling

Bard's Play to Undergo Renovation by Bernstein, Robbins and Laurents

The signal success of musicalized Shakespeare, as exemplified by "Kiss Me Kate" . . . may very well have set a fashion for future Broadway stage offerings.

The latest song and dance project drawing its inspiration from a work of the Bard's is a modern musical drama, as yet untitled, based on "Romeo and Juliet." Involved in getting it on the local boards are none other than Leonard Bernstein, the well-known pianist-composer-conductor, Arthur Laurents, author of "Home of the Brave," and Jerome Robbins, the choreographer. . . . The producing auspices have not been determined yet, but the matter is expected to be settled within a week. According to the present scheme of things, the musical will arrive in New York next season.

—*The New York Times*, January 27, 1949

The announcement was extremely optimistic and vastly premature. One of several problems with the concept—tentatively titled *East Side Story*—lay with its two opposing forces. Jewish-Catholic conflict had been an acknowledged problem for so many years that it had long ago turned into the butt of jokes. Even worse, it had been the subject matter for *Abie's Irish Rose*, the 1922 Broadway comedy that was legendary for scoring record-breaking success despite terrible reviews. There were also, among the three collaborators, a number of personal conflicts. Besides being the same age and from similar backgrounds, Robbins, Bernstein, and Laurents shared much in common: all were fiercely intelligent, intense, ambitious, volatile, egotistical, and gay. (Bernstein and Robbins practiced what might be designated an extremely complicated bisexuality.) Such a combination of talents could clearly make for great art, and also for a cacophonous and often toxic combustibility. Bernstein was as mercurial as his music; Laurents was a master at clever, cutting sarcasm; and Robbins's outbursts of temper, on professional and sometimes personal fronts, promptly became the stuff of legend. The ballerina Nora Kaye, a friend to all three men, predicted, "You'll never write it. Your three temperaments in one room, and the walls will come down." So it was, and in an act of hibernation, not extermination, the three collaborators moved on to other work, relegating *East Side Story* to a position well beyond that of a back burner.

Cut to six years later. Even before Bernstein and Laurents had that light-bulb moment with the San Bernardino killing, the overlapping topics of gang violence and juvenile delinquency were finding greater currency in the news and in everyday life. With the new sound of rock 'n' roll as a jangling accompaniment, the entire concept of the American teenager was changing radically. Teens were becoming both the audience and subject for an increasing amount of popular culture. Films like *Blackboard Jungle* (1955) and *Rebel Without a Cause* (1955) reflected their lives with a rough-edged kind of glamour and romance. It was also beginning to be clear that the conflicts arising between rival teen gangs were based less in religion than in ethnicity. When Laurents proposed to Bernstein that there might be a way to revive *East Side Story*, they took their cue from the California stories and changed its hostilities from Jews versus Catholics to Latinos against Anglos. It soon became still more specific for these two New Yorkers: the gangs then active on Manhattan's West Side, with recent arrivals from Puerto Rico opposing the descendants of earlier immigrants from Europe.

Subject matter this timely and grave was well off any beaten path for musical theater. If the Rodgers and Hammerstein shows had been serious, they were set long ago (*Oklahoma!*, *Carousel*) or far off (*South Pacific, The King and I*). And when had a mature piece of musical theater been set only blocks away from where it was being performed? Yes, *Guys and Dolls* took place in Times Square, but it was funny. This was not, and its cast would be comprised almost entirely of young people, with a few incidental, mostly ineffectual, adults. Moreover, these teenagers were involved in matters more critical than puppy love or making a success in show business. Not simply weighty but outright dire: the first-act curtain came down on two corpses. This seemed to be the territory of *Hamlet*, not *The Pajama Game*.

At the same time they were negotiating this fresh and risky territory, Robbins, Bernstein, and Laurents were also attending to a densely varied group of obligations. Ever a whirlwind of artistry, Bernstein was composing his musical play *Candide*, developing programs for the TV series *Omnibus*, and conducting a series of concerts at Carnegie Hall. Laurents was working on the play *A Clearing in the Woods* and on the screenplay of *Anastasia* (1956). Robbins was choreographing the film version of *The King and I* (1956) and staging the Broadway hit *Bells Are Ringing*. Amid all this, they continued to collaborate and correspond about the new work, eventually in the company of a fourth team member. Stephen Sondheim, only in his midtwenties, was a writer and composer with limited professional credits but also unlimited potential. While Bernstein originally planned on writing the lyrics himself, he was too occupied with other projects to do so. Sondheim, for his part, would also have preferred to write both words and music, yet was not established enough to

ROBERT E. GRIFFITH and HAROLD S. PRINCE

(By arrangement with ROGER L. STEVENS)

present

A new musical

West Side Story

Based on a conception of Jerome Robbins

Book by **ARTHUR LAURENTS**

Music by **LEONARD BERNSTEIN**

Lyrics by **STEPHEN SONDHEIM**

with

CAROL LAWRENCE • LARRY KERT • CHITA RIVERA • ART SMITH

Mickey Calin • Ken LeRoy • Lee Becker • David Winters • Tony Mordente • Eddie Roll • Grover Dale

Entire Production Directed and Choreographed by

JEROME ROBBINS

Scenic Production by **OLIVER SMITH** Costumes Designed by **IRENE SHARAFF** Lighting by **JEAN ROSENTHAL**

Co-Choreographer **PETER GENNARO** Production Associate **SYLVIA DRULIE**

Musical Direction MAX GOBERMAN Orchestrations by LEONARD BERNSTEIN with SID RAMIN and IRWIN KOSTAL

WINTER GARDEN

BROADWAY AT 50th STREET MATS. WED. & SAT.

ABOVE: A rehearsal shot of Jerome Robbins in action

be entrusted with such a high-profile job. He took the job as lyricist upon the advice of his mentor, Oscar Hammerstein II, and Bernstein did end up writing some of the lyrics himself (including "One Hand, One Heart") without credit.

As Bernstein and Sondheim tackled the songs, Laurents worked on one script draft after another, all the while getting input, often contentiously and usually brilliantly, from Robbins. The move from Verona balconies to Manhattan fire escapes took comparatively little ingenuity; the greater challenge lay in finding convincing modern counterparts for the characters and situations. The two central figures, Tony and Maria, were the easiest, and it fanned out from there. Juliet's cousin Tybalt became Maria's brother Bernardo, and her suitor Paris was

Chino, Maria's arranged fiancé. Mercutio, Romeo's raffish best friend, turned into Riff. Shakespeare's adults, meanwhile, were largely eliminated. The sympathetic Doc was a scaled-down version of Friar Laurence, and apart from him there was only the presence of the unfeeling and unseeing police. The Montagues and Capulets were translated into the two gangs, the Jets and the Sharks, with their male fighting members and supportive girlfriends. The most inventive reconfiguration came with Juliet's Nurse, who became Anita—slightly older than Maria, quite a bit more worldly, a reluctant and eventually poignant intermediary. Maria's ultimate fate was the cause of intense discussions. Should she, too, be a victim of the opposing forces? Or, as with Juliet, a suicide? Finally, they determined that she would be alive at the finale, delivering a blistering rebuke to the gangs and their culture of violence. There was no final Shakespearean message of conciliation. Viewers inclined toward optimism could hope that the carnage, and Maria's anger-infused grief, might lead to a kind of peace. There did, however, remain those gang members on both sides who hang back when others unite to carry off Tony's body.

The treatment was as unconventional as the subject matter. Where most musicals opened with an overture, here the curtain rose in silence on a grim cityscape. Then began Robbins's remarkable Prologue, a kind of vivid recap of the long-standing animosity between the Jets and the Sharks. After that, everything proceeded seamlessly, its integration of movement and music not at all like the "dialog/cue/song/dance" pattern of most musicals. Even the standouts among the songs seemed more subtle than the usual showstoppers. (One, called "Like Everybody Else," was deleted because of its resemblance to conventional musical comedy.) The script was notably spare, with much of the drama presented through means other than spoken words. When the gangs meet in the gym, for example, their animosity was portrayed not with dialog or conventional action but through competitive dance. Likewise, Tony and Maria's first meeting was depicted wordlessly, with Robbins's direction and Bernstein's music making it appear that time and enmity had momentarily stopped. Less verbiage, more drama.

Bernstein's *Candide*, glorious as it was, had been a failure in part because the direction was not in sync with the material. Here, everything would be in alignment, with Robbins ensuring that the momentum of the drama equaled that of the music. "Something's Coming" (the last song to be added before tryouts) had an urgent propulsion, "Maria" evoked love-at-first-sight rapture, and in "Tonight" the spirit of both songs merged in an ecstatic duet. "Gee, Officer Krupke," whose melody Bernstein recycled from a *Candide* castoff, modified the old tropes of vaudeville comedy into a newer and harsher context. There was also comedy in "America," as borne on its complex rhythms, and "Cool" had the jazz to fit its title. Although Sondheim later fretted about some of the lyrics in "I Feel Pretty," the song worked perfectly as a small ray of sunshine and optimism, and "Somewhere" conveyed longing and aspiration while steering clear of false hope or platitudes. Bernstein's dance music, too, was different. In many musicals, the dances were set to instrumental reworkings of their songs. Here, Bernstein wrote the dances as new pieces, some of them so intricate that the dancers occasionally had difficulty keeping count. A few years later, they became Bernstein's much-performed concert piece "Symphonic Dances from *West Side Story*."

By the spring of 1957, the project was known by its working title *Gangway* (sometimes with an exclamation point) and was assuming its final form. The production team

was of the highest possible quality: producers Roger Stevens, Robert Griffith, and Harold Prince, set designer Oliver Smith, costumer Irene Sharaff, and lighting designer Jean Rosenthal, with Robbins as director and choreographer. Assembling a cast took a long six months, with countless auditions and callbacks made necessary by nearly unprecedented requirements: performers with training and experience who looked (or were) young enough to be convincing teenagers, possessed the ability to sing intricate music, and could dance *really* well. Carol Lawrence, for whom an endless round of repeat auditions became something of an ordeal, was a Maria who could sing beautifully, look believable, act sensitively, and move with grace. Larry Kert encompassed both Tony's toughness as a former gang leader and his sensitivity as a young man in love plus, again, the ability to both look and sound exactly right. Most of the performers cast as Puerto Rican characters reflected the conventions of the time by being mostly non-Hispanic, with Chita Rivera as the most conspicuous exception. Down the line, all the roles were cast with dancer-actor-singers who could blossom under the Jerome Robbins brand of leadership: smart, rigorous, and tough.

As the main person in charge, Robbins commanded rapt attention and fear-

TOP: Maria and Tony on Broadway: Larry Kert and Carol Lawrence in the balcony scene

BOTTOM: The Rumble on Broadway: Mickey Calin and Ken LeRoy

ful respect. He was aware that, unlike *Bells Are Ringing*, this work truly mattered. His demands were unrelenting and his outbursts frequent, yet he became known to the cast as "Big Daddy," which connotes both paternalism and perhaps fear. The dancers, for the most part, were intensely devoted to him; his Anita, Chita Rivera, put it this way: "I just loved him so much. He's responsible for so much of whatever there is that's professional and good about me in the theater. I used to say that if Big Daddy had told me to jump off a building's fourth story and land on my left foot in plié, I would know it's possible because he could never steer me wrong."

Some others were not as taken with his approach, and it was a generally accepted truism that in any Robbins show at least one cast member was singled out for abuse. As a former dancer, he was accustomed to pushing hard, which for him meant that feelings and limitations, even possible breaking points, did not necessarily matter. What might be inspired guidance for one performer could be, for another, intolerable. Some, like Carole D'Andrea (Velma), refused to acknowledge the hectoring. Others had more problems, and Robbins was especially rough with Kert and with his Riff, Mickey Calin (later known as Michael Callan). Some of the harshness was calculated: Robbins, who had studied at the Actors Studio, took a Method-style approach to deepen the performers' identification with their roles. He often rehearsed the Jets and the Sharks

separately and demanded that they not mix—the better to foster a sense of competitiveness. As he intended, this added to the show's intensity. It also, occasionally, made for outright hostility.

Many performers' attitudes toward Robbins were made still more complicated by some recent political history. In 1953, he had "named names" to the voraciously anti-Communist House Un-American Activities Committee, which resulted the blacklisting of seven of his associates. This, for many members of the New York theater community, was difficult to forgive and harder to forget. Much later, Robbins himself confessed that the fear driving him to turn in some of his associates stemmed less from being revealed as a former Communist than being exposed as homosexual. For some, the episode enhanced the notion that Robbins was an artist to be simultaneously revered and despised.

One famous anecdote associated with Robbins is so lethally evocative that it seems almost mythical. Accounts have differed about where it originated, yet several sources have testified that it occurred during *West Side Story*, specifically during the show's second round of tryouts in Philadelphia. It goes this way: At one point during a rehearsal, Robbins lost his temper completely and embarked on what was, even for him, a major tirade. Standing with his back to the auditorium, he directed his loud dissatisfaction to everyone on the stage. They were doing it wrong, they were incompetent, clueless, inept, idiotic. They were, in sum, a disgrace to the show, to the entertainment industry, most likely to the entire world. Continuing his attack, he began to slowly back away, as if in revulsion, from the objects of his fury. They, unlike Robbins, could see that he was moving dangerously close to the edge of the stage. No one said a word as he plunged backward off the stage into the orchestra pit, where the only thing that prevented him from serious injury was a strategically positioned bass drum. Later on the performers could only wonder: Had they all kept quiet because they thought he would stop in time? Had they been mesmerized into silence? Was it due to loathing, uncertainty, or vengeance? Perhaps a kind of terrified dread? None of them really knew.

It remains an incontrovertible fact, as well, that during *West Side Story*—show and film—and afterward, many of the dancers who Robbins directed and sometimes terrorized remained devoted to him. Long after his death in 1998, they continued to speak of him with awe and often love, yet not hesitating to recall the rigors and occasional agony of working with him.

Late in rehearsals, the title was changed from *Gangway!* to *West Side Story*. Finally, as did nearly every musical of the time, the show went out of town for tryouts. There was still some tweaking and fine-tuning to do—not a surprise, given the trademarked Robbins perfectionism—yet notably less than in other major productions. The curtain first came up on *West Side Story* on August 19, 1957, in Washington, D.C., and the impact was immediate. The second tryout city was Philadelphia, which was notoriously tough on Broadway-bound shows. Even there, some good reviews lifted everyone up prior to the main event: Thursday, September 26, 1957, at the Winter Garden Theatre, 1634 Broadway.

As with the tale of Robbins's "taking the plunge," the opening night of *West Side Story* has passed into legend. Some accounts go so far as to allege that it changed the entire history of musical theater forever, which is perhaps a little much. What is certain is that the show began in a way both riveting and unexpected: the curtain rising in silence on Oliver Smith's grimly stylized urban landscape, a group of blue-jacketed Jets posed tensely. Then the first sound—not music, but finger-snapping—as the Jets began to move. Then, suddenly, another gang, the Sharks, followed by an outbreak of gang warfare, seemingly chaotic but tightly controlled. Finally, the music entered, its sporty dissonance both a provocation and a commentary. Eventually, there was the interruption of a whistle and some police, whose entrance seemed less a remedy than a potential incitement. Although Robbins's Prologue had taken only a few minutes, it defined the entire show, and it was one of the triumphs of the evening that the rest did not seem anticlimactic. Every scene, every song, all the performances, seemed to emanate from that virtuoso opening. It would not be a work of unrelieved tension, for there was lyricism,

ABOVE: The final scene: Jamie Sanchez (far left), Carol Lawrence, and Larry Kert

PAGES 22-23: Anita goes to Doc's: Chita Rivera and the Jets

comedy, rapture, even some overtones (as with "Krupke") of conventional musical comedy. Yet there was an underlying feeling of foreboding, a darkness that seldom seemed far away. The animosity portrayed in *Romeo and Juliet* had been between two wealthy families, and as deep-seated as it was, it was less cultural and sociological than personal. By contrast, *West Side Story* presented an ongoing crisis, new in its torn-from-the-headlines specifics yet wearyingly similar to other ethnic conflicts before and since. It was raw, pertinent, and unpleasant, and neither this show's gifted creators nor anyone else could provide any easy solutions. Or, perhaps, any solutions at all.

A number of cast members later recalled the silence on September 26, after the Jets

and the Sharks carried off Tony's body and the last Bernstein chords played. As Carol Lawrence remembered it, it was a quiet so pervasive as to make the cast feel confused and confounded. Momentarily, it seemed that there was no audience reaction at all, that the show had just taken place before a mass of cold air. "Oh God," Lawrence thought, "They hated it! They didn't get it. They didn't understand what we were trying to say." Then, suddenly, everyone rose, so quickly and immediately as to seem choreographed. Then came the sound, the applause and the cheers that went on and on and on. Yells, stomping, weeping even, all well beyond the electrical charge that traditionally attends the opening of a worthy new show. It was a reaction as different from traditional applause as *West Side*

Story was from the other shows playing on Broadway at the same time. The long lines promptly began to form at the Winter Garden box office.

The audience enthusiasm did not translate unreservedly to the critical community. It's well known that *West Side Story* did not generate universal raves after it opened, to the point that it has become a signal example of a major work that audiences may have comprehended ahead of critics. In 1957, the many daily newspapers in New York included some names that later faded away, such as the *Herald Tribune*, the *World-Telegram and Sun*, the *Daily Mirror*, and the *Journal American*. Each had theater critics with opinions that carried weight with the public, and some had very positive things to say: "Extraordinarily exciting" (*Daily News*); "A sensational hit!" (*Daily Mirror*); "The most exciting thing that has come to town since *My Fair Lady*" (*Journal American*). Some praised the show in its entirety as a breakthrough new work, and many singled out Robbins as the first among equals.

Many, too, responded favorably to Bernstein's music, although the *Times* music critic, Howard Taubman, judged the score "disappointing," particularly in its effort to span the divide between musical theater and opera. Even when there was enthusiasm about the music, there was not necessarily understanding, as in one approving review that termed the show "a juke-box Manhattan opera." There was also the related, if confounding, opinion of some that the music did not provide enough in the way of "hummable" tunes. The songs that most proved the inaccuracy of this claim, "Tonight," "Maria," "I Feel Pretty," and "Somewhere," all had to wait a while before entering the roster of standards. It's worth noting that, in all the discussion of the music and the songs, Stephen Sondheim's name appeared seldom, if ever.

The initial notices also included a wary but enthusiastic "money review" from the dean of New York theater critics. Brooks Atkinson, of the *Times*, was one of those legendary figures with the power to make or break a show with one paragraph, so respected/feared that a Broadway theater later took his name. He could not begin without a confession of some mixed feelings: "Although the material is horrifying, the workmanship is admirable." He went on, in a positive vein. "Everything . . . is of a piece. Everything contributes to the total impression of wildness, ecstasy, and anguish." It was, he concluded, "one of those occasions where theatre people, engrossed in an original project, are all in top form."

Atkinson was not alone in his reservation about the subject matter; other critics considered it a significant roadblock. Some of this feeling sprang, one way or another, from Shakespeare. Even before the show opened, it had become known as "the modern *Romeo and Juliet* musical," and for a critic such as the respected Walter Kerr, writing in the *Herald Tribune*, the script's connection with its source was, in some ways, insufficient.

"It is, apart from the spine-tingling velocity of the dances, almost never emotionally affecting," he wrote. "Perhaps these teen-age gangsters are too ferocious, too tawdry, too intent upon grinding their teeth to interest us compassionately. . . ." Kerr's review hit on another objection as well, which can be sensed in his use of the words "tawdry" and "compassionately." Simply put, the Jets and the Sharks and their world were not necessarily felt to deserve this level of attention and quality. Wolcott Gibbs, in the *New Yorker*, was even more explicit in calling out the perceived unworthiness of the subject, declaring that he could not "believe that significant tragedy [can] exist among juvenile delinquents." This perceived "unsuitability" of the subject matter was a criticism frequently directed at *West Side Story* in its earliest years. Later, due in part to the impact of the film version, such disapproval was registered less and less.

Another objection that began to surface even before opening night marked the starting point for problems with the show that would mount later on. In the Sunday *Times* of September 29, 1957 the nationally recognized physician Howard Rusk related that a number of Puerto Rican people, both on the island itself and in New York, were protesting one individual line: the lyric in "America" that termed Puerto Rico an "island of tropic diseases." As he noted the achievement of the show in general and Sondheim's lyrics in particular, Dr. Rusk called the offending phrase "a blow below the belt." To make

his point, he stated that malaria in Puerto Rico had been all but eradicated, and that recent numbers showed the island's overall death rate to have declined dramatically. In conclusion, Rusk pointedly noted that New York City should fare as well with controlling juvenile delinquency as Puerto Rico did with disease. Following Dr. Rusk's cue, Sondheim indeed changed the lyrics when it came time for the film version. Otherwise, in 1950s Broadway as in 1960s Hollywood, ethnic and cultural sensitivity were not a dominant force.

For about three months after its premiere, *West Side Story* was Broadway's go-to hit, embraced by well-off intellectuals, the theater-savvy, and that portion of the public who tended to flock to every high-profile show. (People could do so more economically back then: the ticket prices ranged from balcony seats at $2.50 to front orchestra at $8.05, approximately one-twentieth of what they are now.) While the standing room sign was posted frequently in those early months, it soon became clear that this was not an all-encompassing juggernaut on the order of *My Fair Lady*, which was still turning away people more than a year after it opened. That kind of audience-pleaser arrived on December 19, and it was titled *The Music Man*. Set in a small Iowa town in 1912, it extolled traditional values, celebrated a scoundrel's reformation, and offered music—song, dance, and instrumental—as an irresistible cure for countless ills. Where *West Side Story* offered spiky challenge, *The Music Man* bestowed

warmth and high spirits. "Gary, Indiana" instead of "America," barbershop quartets instead of gangs, a blissful ending at the final curtain rather than a death procession and the feeling that there may be more to follow. Two faces of musical theater, both valid, both vital and lovingly wrought, both necessary and, ultimately, classic. One looked to the past with love; the other to the present in its theme, and to the future in its creative daring. There were also, in that supposedly pre–"divided America" time, some major political and social contrasts. The Iowa of *The Music Man* was a place of homogenization, with nary a nonwhite face; conversely, *West Side Story* based much of its conflict on ethnic clash. In a 1957–58 Broadway season, it was all but preordained which one scored the greater popular success and captured most of that year's Tony Awards.

Few major Broadway musicals of that time were not then made into films, although Broadway and Hollywood had seldom enjoyed a pleasant relationship. Far too many shows had been slashed, distorted, miscast, or dumbed-down on their way to the screen, and it was well known that producers tended to look down on movies even as they were willing to accept the cash. The income from film adaptations became more plentiful after 1946, when MGM paid a lofty $600,000 for the rights to Irving Berlin's *Annie Get Your Gun*. Later, it reached a heart-stopping climax when the rights to *My Fair Lady* sold to Warner Bros. for $5.5 million plus a share of gross profits. Forget

about just the rights: this amount was more than *the total cost* of almost every film ever made before the early 1960s. *The Music Man*, for its part, was sold to movies for a cool million.

In contrast, and as it did with just about everything, *West Side Story* took a different path. In July of 1958 it was announced that the film rights had been sold not to a large studio but to an enterprising new independent company, Seven Arts Productions. The price was a startlingly low $350,000, with an additional 10 percent of the world gross after the film recouped its cost. Additionally, Bernstein and Sondheim agreed to an option wherein they would (for a joint $7,500) write three new songs, if the producers desired. As if to make this all seem even more nominal, Seven Arts also bought the rights to another show currently on Broadway, *Two for the Seesaw*. The price for that two-character comedy-drama was $600,000 plus percentage . . . and the work with the lower price tag turned out to be the one with vastly greater staying power. The news of the film sale was, at any rate, something of a false start, or perhaps it might be termed an overture. Seven Arts, although its name remained on the movie credits due to contractual considerations, was soon out of the picture entirely.

Why did the rights for *West Side Story* go for a pittance in comparison to those for *My Fair Lady*? In two words: perceived appeal. Movie producers were afraid of *West Side Story*, doubting any potential it might have to achieve financial success with a wide audience. Even on Broadway, it did not run nearly as long as a number of its less challenging contemporaries—under two years, as opposed to *The Music Man*'s run of well over three years and *My Fair Lady*'s record tally of six-plus. The crowds thrilled by *West Side Story*—the ones Carol Lawrence saw and heard at the premiere—were urban, savvy, open to innovative presentation and provocative themes. Those out seeking simpler amusement went, by and large, to other shows that were, to put it plainly, less of a downer. *West Side Story* told a sad and difficult story about people who most audience members did not want to meet—people who hated and killed each other. Nor, by the time of its closing curtain, were matters set aright. This was something that discerning theater audiences could accept for a fixed amount of time, while—then and now—the shows that run the longest are the ones with more "popular" inducements, the ones that the visitors flock to see after the New Yorkers have moved on. The low price of the film rights was also connected to the wobbly and sometimes nonexistent track record movie musicals had in confronting offbeat or "highbrow" themes. There was no guarantee that this one, as filmed, could be able to come through the Hollywood maw intact, and Bernstein's music was not judged to have the instant appeal of tunes by a Richard Rodgers or Irving Berlin. The Robbins dances, for their part, bore no resemblance to anything in any previous musical. Being a work of

quality and distinction did not necessarily ensure its commercial success.

One of the few ways to guarantee the film's financial viability would be to come up with a box-office "name," and that did not seem likely. It followed, logically, that casting did indeed end up as one of the thorniest and most demanding issues befalling *West Side Story* on its move to the screen. This journey ended up taking significantly less time than the eight-plus years of gestation prior to Broadway, but less time does not mean less conflict. On the contrary.

ABOVE: Broadway's first Anita and Maria: Chita Rivera and Carol Lawrence on Broadway

CHAPTER TWO

MIRACLE DUE: PLANNING A MOVIE

—

"Let us take the image, the soul, the spirit of *West Side Story* and retell it our own way."

BORIS LEVEN
Production Designer

ABOVE: Production designer Boris Leven with a model for Maria's fire escape

PAGE 26: Codirectors: Jerome Robbins and Robert Wise

IT WOULD ONLY BE WORTH DOING if it were as arresting and innovative on film as it had been in the theater. Unlike previous movies that used a New York setting as a backdrop, this one was going to feature the grim, unyielding, poverty-stricken Manhattan that out-of-towners never saw. Its romance was tragic, its humor hard-edged and even bitter, and there was a good deal more sexual passion than song-and-dance pieces were usually willing to invoke. As for juvenile delinquency: movies had begun to broach the subject with some honesty in productions such as *Blackboard Jungle*, but that was not a musical. Above all, it could never be forgotten that the whole premise of

West Side Story had its basis in ethnic animosity.

Even the basic musical ingredients were not akin to anything in previous films. Bernstein's score, with its tensions, dissonance, and rhythmic lunges, was nothing like standard movie tune-writing—which is also why the only Bernstein show filmed up to then, *On the Town* (1949), lost most of its songs in the transition from stage to screen. (Judging them too sophisticated for a mass audience, producer Arthur Freed had them replaced with non-Bernstein pieces that could never be subject to that accusation.) Sondheim's lyrics, for their part, balanced more conventional elements, as in "Tonight," with intricate rhymes and some quite pointed social commentary. Then there was the dancing. If a film like *An American in Paris* (1951) was acclaimed for taking choreography far past its previous cinematic limits, *West Side Story* exceeded that standard by a fair distance. Aside from the daunting challenge the dances posed technically, there was also the issue of believability: How does a director build a bridge from plot to dance? The sheer act of photographing dance is a complicated business. It requires a director with a firm and coherent vision, plus the awareness that one cannot simply park the camera, cue the music, and hope for the best.

One helpful guide for the filmmakers came with a quick look at the musical shows filmed just prior to *West Side Story*. For the most part, they furnished a tidy demonstration of what the film could *not* be, as well as the wobbly state of movie musicals in general. *South Pacific* (1958) was a hit mainly because people loved the show and the music so much that they were willing to disregard the many reviews that took issue with the way it had been put on the screen. *Porgy and Bess* (1959), a major flop, was static and misguided, costing more than any previous musical and ending the career of its producer, Samuel Goldwyn. *Lil' Abner* (1959) was an amusing live-action comic strip and *Bells Are Ringing* (1960) was a nice vehicle for Judy Holliday; while entertaining, neither had much impact with the public. As for *Can-Can* (1960), few critics found it worthy of the prestige treatment Twentieth Century-Fox tried to bestow upon it, and it failed to make back its sizable cost.

Compare these to the films of the time that audiences were lining up to see: *Some Like It Hot* (1959), *The Apartment* (1960), and *Psycho* (1960), all of them immediate, daring, and dynamic. They were products of a changing Hollywood, which by 1960 was beginning to witness untold upheaval. Most crucially, the old studio system, in place for forty years, was beginning its journey to both the poorhouse and the morgue. Times, tastes, and demographics had all changed, television had turned everything upside down, and the entire natures of moviemaking and moviegoing were undergoing an immense shake-up. A film of *West Side Story*, were it to have any kind of artistic or commercial impact, needed to reflect something of this coming new tide. It could not settle for studio-sealed complacency nor for excessive compromise.

As history would have it, *West Side Story* did not end up as the product of a movie studio. Not, at least, in the conventional sense of the term "studio." United Artists, founded in 1919, was around the same age as the other movie companies, yet operated in a very different fashion from MGM, Universal, Paramount, or Fox. Those were big-studio factories, while United Artists existed largely on paper as a supervised and ever-changing consortium of independent companies and producers. Instead of a "big-tent" kind of production hierarchy, each company and producer essentially acquired their own properties and rented their own studio facilities, while United Artists financed the projects, handled their distribution, and took a share of the profits.

This setup had many variances through the years, but its general through line was that most of the films, good or otherwise, were the products of a hands-on production team as opposed to the studio assembly line. By 1960, such a system was proving increasingly advantageous, while the old studios, with their bloated payrolls and high overhead, were beginning to tank. A good deal of this prosperity at United Artists was coming through the efforts of three brothers named Mirisch.

The Mirisch Company achieved its success the hard way. In 1945, young Walter Mirisch, who had studied business at Harvard, began his film career at Monogram Pictures. Monogram, the home of the Bowery Boys, microbudgeted westerns, and *Black Market Babies* (1945), was cinema at its most hardscrabble, so poverty-stricken that it had no sound department and had to rent cameras because it couldn't afford to buy them. Mirisch began at Monogram as a general assistant, learned the ropes quickly, and in less than two years became a full-fledged producer. By the 1950s, he was the production head, his brother Harold was company vice president, and Monogram had changed its name to Allied Artists. Then, in 1957, came the big step: Walter and Harold Mirisch, along with their half brother Marvin, formed the Mirisch Company, an independent organization producing films for

OPPOSITE: The Mirisch brothers: Walter, Harold, and Marvin

release by United Artists. The initial Mirisch productions, like *Fort Massacre* (1958) and *The Gunfight at Dodge City* (1959), were almost a throwback to Monogram. Then, in Walter Mirisch's words, "Billy Wilder told us that he was interested in doing a film about an all-girl orchestra." The resulting smash of *Some Like It Hot* instantly marked the fledgling company as one of the industry's leading independent production groups.

It was shortly after *Some Like It Hot* began to draw large crowds that the Mirisch Company became involved with *West Side Story*. Originally, the film rights had been sold to Seven Arts Productions, another independent company under the United Artists umbrella. United Artists had provided the financing for that sale, plus the rights for the play *Two for the Seesaw* and the novel *By Love Possessed*. Not long after that, Seven Arts and United Artists parted ways, leaving UA with three expensive and diverse properties in need of a production company. The Mirisch Company got the call and, after flying to New York to see both plays, Walter Mirisch declared *West Side Story* to be one of the most exciting pieces of theater he'd ever experienced. He returned to California with two notions in particular: that Jerome Robbins must be involved with a *West Side Story* film, and that Billy Wilder should direct *Two for the Seesaw*. Wilder quickly passed in favor of another idea he was developing. That became *The Apartment*, a second Wilder-Mirisch triumph and another demonstration of the advantages of independent filmmaking: personal, detailed, adult and, in this case, better. It was also fast, running on movie screens long before *West Side Story* and the two other former Seven Arts projects. All three—*West Side Story, Two for the Seesaw* (1962), and *By Love Possessed* (1961)—clearly required far more preparation and, of the trio, only *West Side Story* emerged as a success.

As Walter Mirisch had been quick to observe, Jerome Robbins was essential to *West Side Story*. However much he had carried on during the show's inception, arguing with Bernstein and Laurents over billing and ownership, and however hard he had pushed the cast, his imprint was indelible. The show was *his* artistic statement. What audiences experienced on the stage of the Winter Garden Theatre was what Robbins put there, in look and movement, in dramatic and musical flow, in mood and momentum. Without him, a movie version might go the way of *On Your Toes* (1939) or *Pal Joey* (1957), outstanding shows that lost most of their dance when filmed. Robbins knew and understood *West Side Story* better than anyone, but he also had precious little experience with movies. His credits, in fact, numbered exactly two.

Robbins's film debut practically defines the word "obscure": in 1942, he staged the dances for a Mexican musical called *Yo bailé con don Porfirio* (I Danced with Don Porfirio). His second one, in extreme contrast, was the 1956 film version of *The King and I.* Having choreographed the show on Broadway, he repeated and refined much of his work and

ABOVE: Jerome Robbins working on *The King and I* in 1956. From left, Robbins, music director Alfred Newman, Rita Moreno, and Yul Brynner

OPPOSITE: Four of the film's chief creators look at a preliminary set model: Jerome Robbins, Robert Wise, associate producer Saul Chaplin, and production designer Boris Leven.

was responsible for possibly its most striking sequence. "The Small House of Uncle Thomas" is a mesmerizing ballet that retells *Uncle Tom's Cabin* in Southeast Asian terms, by way of Broadway, and is unlike any other dance in any film. It's a planet, or at least a hemisphere, away from *West Side Story*, yet the two works share some common ground: difficult or offbeat subject matter, fierce commitment on the part of both the director and the performers, expressive and tightly controlled physical movement, and a theatrical artificiality that, paradoxically, plays well on film. That "Uncle Thomas" and "Cool" were the product of one director's creative imagination seems next to unimaginable. Then

again, that was Robbins. Saul Chaplin, associate producer of *West Side Story*, said:

The only person I've ever met that I'm *positive* is a genius is Jerome Robbins. If you know him, you cannot come to any other conclusion. I know Lenny Bernstein very well, I know a lot of others. They're enormously talented, true, but Robbins is a genius. That's it. As a genius, it makes him very difficult to work with, and if you're willing to put up with that, fine.

Mirisch was willing to put up with that. Nevertheless, he was aware that entrusting the entire film to Robbins or any first-time director could be folly. He decided to go with the notion, unconventional but not unprecedented, of having two directors, Robbins alongside someone with film experience. There are a few examples of this being done successfully: the producer-writer-director team of Michael Powell and Emeric Pressburger, responsible for such important British films as *The Red Shoes* (1948) and *Black Narcissus* (1947); and, much later, the sibling teams of Joel and Ethan Coen, Bobby and Peter Farrelly, and Lana and Lilly [formerly Larry and Andy] Wachowski. The director's role could be somewhat different in musicals. The general procedure was to have a director shoot the "plot" scenes and a choreographer stage the musical sequences. Sometimes the director could supervise the shooting of the musical numbers, sometimes not; Robbins had accomplished his work on *The King and I* with minimal input from the credited director Walter Lang.

Something different, and quite glorious, came with the pairing of Gene Kelly and Stanley Donen. Both had been trained as dancers, and when Kelly was called on to come up with dance sequences for *Cover Girl* (1944) and *Anchors Aweigh* (1945), Donen worked with him. The results were so outstanding that MGM allowed them to co-direct *On the Town*, a Robbins-Bernstein collaboration on Broadway that was successfully reconceived for film. They followed this with the immortal *Singin' in the Rain*, and with *It's Always Fair Weather* (1955). Kelly and Donen's was a true collaboration, albeit sometimes contentious and complicated. (Such things can happen when two coworkers marry the same woman at different times.) Even with their disagreements, they created three first-rate films in which the interconnection of song, dance, and script mattered greatly. *West Side Story* required that connectivity as well, for its music and dance were not only essential but *inherent*. Everything needed to be linked aurally, visually, through movement and color, and using every other device at a director's disposal. Robbins knew how to make this happen on the stage but, Mirisch understood, not on film. Someone with a filmmaker's vocabulary needed to work alongside him, while at the same time ensuring that the collaboration emerged as the product of a unified vision.

The solution, for codirector, came in Robert Wise, who was already discussing a production deal with Mirisch. Wise entered the business while still in his teens, and by his midtwenties had become a film editor

ABOVE: Robbins's ballet, "The Small House of Uncle Thomas," in *The King and I*

with major credits. The 1939 version of *The Hunchback of Notre Dame* was his, as was the epochal *Citizen Kane* (1941). The director's chair was the next stop, and Wise's work spanned a wide variety of genres and moods: tough realism (*The Set-Up*, 1949); hard-boiled film noir (*Born to Kill*, 1947); science fiction (*The Day the Earth Stood Still*, 1951); psychological western (*Blood on the Moon*, 1948); war film (*The Desert Rats*, 1953); spectacle (*Helen of Troy*, 1956); biography (*Somebody Up There Likes Me*, 1956); social protest (*I Want to Live!*, 1958); and, most recently, the violent crime drama *Odds Against Tomorrow* (1959). About the only genre missing from the Wise résumé was the musical; the closest he had come was *This Could Be the Night* (1957), an amiable comedy set in a nightclub, which featured moments of music

and dance. While that had been a financial failure, Wise's success rate remained very high and, along with his versatility, he had a reputation for staying in or under budget. He was known to run a tight ship without resorting to the scare tactics used by certain other directors, and actors generally found that his easygoing approach made for a positive on-set environment. He also had a reputation as a genuinely nice person, neither a prima donna nor a pushover. Perhaps, in some ways, he was the complete opposite of Jerome Robbins. When Mirisch offered him the codirecting job for *West Side Story*, Wise signed on enthusiastically.

The directorial duo thus had both a stable anchor and a brilliant wild card, plus something of a game plan. Robbins would naturally be staging the musical numbers,

including the lead-ins, with input from Wise. Wise was in charge of the "plot" scenes, with input from his codirector. It made sense on paper and in theory, at least until it became clear that each man was developing his own set of ideas, which, it became quite plain, were not necessarily compatible with one another. The Prologue became the first area of contention. For Robbins, it introduced the central conflict in a way that could only be conveyed, as on Broadway, through theatrical means. Wise, who had used locations effectively in earlier films, wanted it shot on genuine New York streets. So did Walter Mirisch. Robbins, Wise later recalled, filed his objection by arguing, "You're giving me the biggest challenge right off the bat. I will take my most stylized dancing [in] the Prologue and put it in the most real background." To which Wise replied, "How is that going to matter?" If this exchange sounds like a case of talking-past-each-other, it is because that's exactly what it was.

With its directorial collaboration off to that interesting start, the production slowly began to come together. Rehearsal and shooting would be at the Samuel Goldwyn Studio at 7200 Santa Monica Boulevard in West Hollywood. Goldwyn, prior to his recent retirement, had already begun to rent out studio space to independent film and television producers—and his studio complex, now modernized and known as The Lot,

TOP: Robert Wise, before *West Side Story*

BOTTOM: Screenwriter Ernest Lehman

serves a similar function to this day. Robert Wise shot *Run Silent, Run Deep* (1958) there in 1957, and the last features made there prior to *West Side Story* were *Porgy and Bess* and Frank Capra's *A Hole in the Head* (1959). Wise, as credited producer, was primarily in charge of most of the personnel and technical decisions, with input from the Mirisches and, soon, Jerome Robbins. The Mirisches oversaw the business side of the production, including budget. Many of the crew members had formerly been under contract to one of the big studios. Now, reflecting the new trend in filmmaking, they were working independently.

For Wise the choice of screenwriter was an easy call: Ernest Lehman, who had been responsible for the scripts of Wise's *Executive Suite* (1954) and *Somebody Up There Likes Me.* Like Wise, Lehman could span genres with ease: his credits also included *Sabrina* (1954), *The King and I*, and *North by Northwest* (1959). He began his work on *West Side Story* by accompanying Wise on a research trip to Manhattan in November of 1959. While Wise scouted possible locations, Lehman spoke with youth board workers and joined the police on a late-night patrol. "Anyone on the street after one AM," a policeman told him, "is either a cop or a robber." As soon as he returned to California, Lehman began work on a series of drafts that retained the tension of the Laurents original while giving some of the characters slightly expanded dimension. In the end, his screenplay adhered closely to the spirit and often

the letter of the stage script while shifting the position of several key moments.

As with all screenwriters, Lehman found his work subject to the strictures and whims of the Motion Picture Association of America. The Association administered that seat of judgment known as the Production Code, the notorious and often puritanical set of moviemaking guidelines. Everything had to pass inspection: the script, costumes, song lyrics, and general theme and tone were all examined and, when necessary, cleaned up. With *West Side Story*, there had been some initial caution involving possible depictions of sex and violence, but by the time Wise submitted the final script for approval, nearly everything was considered acceptable. The main exception came with a couple of lines sung by Anita in the "Tonight Quintet": "Don't matter if he's tired/As long as he's hot." This reference to Bernardo was judged "unacceptably sex-suggestive," and was toned down. The Association also took issue with two references to "social disease" in "Gee, Officer Krupke," but the lyrics stood. As producers had known for a long time, the way to deal with the Code often involved sacrificing one piece in order to keep another. As a result, "Krupke" was ultimately allowed to hold on to its "social disease."

For the all-important musical element, Wise turned to Saul Chaplin, whose credits stretched back to the 1930s. Starting in film as a lyricist, he moved into the role of musical jack-of-all-trades at Columbia Pictures, first on the studio's B-grade features and eventually with important titles such as *Cover Girl* and *The Jolson Story* (1946). His expertise ranged from vocal arrangements to music editing and mixing and still, occasionally, song lyrics. One specialty was his work with singers, including those hired to dub the performers who could not or did not sing for themselves. In 1949, he moved from Columbia to MGM, maker of the biggest and many of the best musicals in the industry. There his credits included *On the Town, An American in Paris, Kiss Me, Kate* (1953), *Seven Brides for Seven Brothers* (1954), *High Society* (1956), and *Les Girls* (1957). Once again, his work at MGM covered numerous bases—vocal arranger, music supervisor, musical director, and eventually associate producer—and it won him two Academy Awards. There was little or nothing about musical filmmaking that Chaplin did not know, and Wise entrusted him with overseeing every aspect of the music. It was the first time that he would be working outside the confines of a large studio.

To conduct Bernstein's brilliantly complicated score, Chaplin knew immediately who he wanted to hire. Johnny Green had also begun as a songwriter ("Body and Soul"), went to work at MGM in 1943, and served as the studio's music director for ten years. He composed, conducted, wrote arrangements, and even appeared on-screen with the MGM studio orchestra in several musical shorts. By general consent, he was one of the most talented musicians working in film. There was only one downside with Green, and it

involved Robert Wise. Normally the soul of patience and diplomacy, Wise could handle just about anyone, except Johnny Green. They had worked together on *Somebody Up There Likes Me*, and Wise hated the experience. He found Green to be unreasonable, demanding, and obnoxious, and the worst part came with the exaggerated accent he used to tell unfunny Borscht Belt–style jokes. Using a tremendous amount of tact and diplomacy, Chaplin was finally able to assure Wise that Green would give him no grief, while at the same time convincing Green that his artistry would not be hindered if he made fewer demands and toned down the shtick. He was so successful in doing this that, eventually, Wise and Green became friends—a testament to both men's professionalism, Green's enormous talent, and the trial-by-fire experience that was the making of *West Side Story*.

Green, as it turned out, emerged as one of the most rock-solid members of the company. This was a particular boon when, after he recorded some of the orchestral tracks, he unwittingly stumbled into some Robbins-vs.-Bernstein hostility. As an old friend of Bernstein's, Green was eager for him to hear the recordings, which sounded sensational. This did not end up being a good idea. To Green's shock, Bernstein hated them and demanded they be rerecorded. His main objection lay with the tempos, which he found to be "abysmally slow." Green was already aware that they were slow—because he had been ordered by Jerome Robbins to

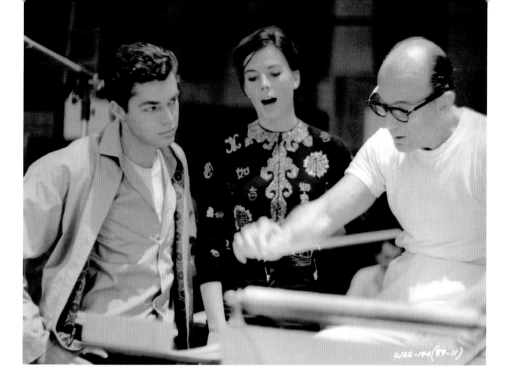

ABOVE: Conductor Johnny Green with Richard Beymer and Natalie Wood

make them that way. There was little that Green and Chaplin could do except reassemble the seventy-two-piece orchestra and redo the recordings with the faster tempos Bernstein insisted upon. Diplomatically, Green did not tell the composer why he had slowed down the music. When Robbins heard the new faster tracks, he accepted them without comment.

Sid Ramin and Irwin Kostal, who had done the orchestrations and musical arrangements for the Broadway production, were called on to repeat their work for film on a considerably expanded scale. The show's orchestra had been, at thirty-one players, unusually large for Broadway, and for movies it was well over double that size. This fact did not sit particularly well with Leonard Bernstein, who preferred a leaner

sound along with faster tempos. Like other New Yorkers shipped out to the West Coast for the first time, Ramin and Kostal were mystified and fascinated by the changes in attitude, climate, and work ethic. Deciding to go with the flow, they set up a card table next to the pool at their hotel, which allowed them to alternate work with the occasional dip. After a slight breeze, they found themselves fishing wet, erased pages out of the water. At that point, Ramin later recalled, "We decided that we should not go Hollywood."

How it all sounded was obviously crucial, and its look needed to carry equal weight. Wise initially had thought about doing an intimately gritty *West Side Story*, shot in the same stark black and white as many of his films, using real locations and keeping everything small-scale. This notion quickly evaporated with the awareness that, as an expensive musical, this production would not be accepted by the viewing public as anything other than big-scale and color. The physical size of the actual film was going to be large as well, since it was to be shot in Panavision 70 (sometimes preceded by the confident adjective "Super"), a new wide-screen process that gave the images unusual sharpness, clarity, and immediacy. The cine-matographer, Daniel L. Fapp, was one of the most respected cameramen in the business, with a long list of credits that included ten of the Dean Martin/Jerry Lewis films, *Lil' Abner*, and *Kings Go Forth* (1958), which starred Frank Sinatra, Tony Curtis, and Natalie Wood. Most recently, he had shot the trouble-plagued Marilyn Monroe musi-cal comedy *Let's Make Love* (1960). On *West Side Story*, his professional competence and authority soon proved to be major assets.

To design the production, Wise turned to Boris Leven, whose recent work had included the hits *Giant* (1956) and *Anatomy of a Murder* (1959). Unlike the theatricality of the original production, Leven designed sets that were strikingly realistic. A more theatrically stylized feeling came with the use of camera angles and editing, lighting and color filters, and judiciously applied special visual effects. Leven's work was aug-mented by that of production artist Maurice "Zuby" Zuberano, whose experience with storyboards extended back to *Citizen Kane*. Leven, Zuberano, and title-credit designer

Saul Bass created storyboards, drawings, and paintings that guided Wise toward some striking color effects and compositions. For Leven and Wise, the collaboration proved so harmonious that they teamed together in the coming decade on five more films, including *The Sound of Music*.

Costume designer Irene Sharaff was the only member of the original Broadway design team to work on the film. Musicals were a specialty for Sharaff, who was best known for elaborate costumes for shows and films like *The King and I* and *An American in Paris*. Her wardrobe for *West Side Story* was deceptively simple. On the surface, these were the clothes of people in their teens and early twenties living in a specific and rundown Manhattan neighborhood. Except for the gym dance, they were street clothes, yet also served as the uniforms for two groups at war with each other. Subtly and ingeniously, Sharaff designed clothes that underscored the conflict between the two factions—subdued earth tones and yellows for the Jets, more intense red and purple and black for the Sharks. Since almost all were dance clothes, functionality was as import-ant as look, They needed to move properly and, in some cases, be nearly skin-tight without threatening to split or come apart. In many cases, the more strenuous numbers required multiple copies.

Two key members of the production team were comparative newcomers. Film editor Thomas Stanford had worked on only one previous feature (*Suddenly, Last*

Summer, 1959), while assistant director Robert Relyea had been in films for five years. In that short time, he had racked up some impressive credits, including *Jailhouse Rock* (1957), Wise's *Until They Sail* (1957), and *The Magnificent Seven* (1960). Also, most formidably, John Wayne's massive *The Alamo* (1960), which had entailed strenuous and exacting work that went well beyond the skill set of most assistant directors. Relyea's tour of duty on *West Side Story* was, if anything, even more rigorous. Not only was he needed to ensure that its two-director setup proceeded harmoniously, he was called on, increasingly, to maintain discipline with unruly cast members. In later years, Relyea recounted the shoot, and its many complications, in quite colorful terms. While many participants had recollections and anecdotes, it is Relyea's that often contain the most hair-raising and mind-boggling detail.

By the spring of 1960, everything was well underway. Lehman was thoughtfully going through multiple drafts of the screenplay, Leven and Sharaff were working on designs and seeing to their execution, Chaplin and Green were working with Ramin and Kostal on the music, and Robbins had begun reconceiving the dances for the camera. Wise was keeping informed of all developments and reporting back to the Mirisch Company, which had approved an initial production budget of approximately $5 million. He was also working intensively on one of the most troublesome aspects of making the film: assembling the right cast.

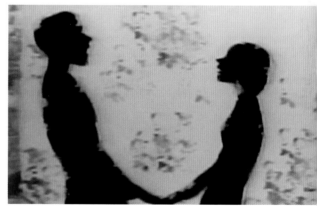

TOP: Irene Sharaff's designs for Teresita, Consuelo, and Rosalia ("Gym Dance" and "America")

BOTTOM: A Maurice Zuberano storyboard sketch for "Tonight"

CHAPTER THREE

LET THEM DO WHAT THEY CAN: FINDING THE CAST

—

"Casting the film proved next to impossible."

SAUL CHAPLIN
Associate Producer

ABOVE: A strong possibility for Tony, Scott Marlowe is on the right, with Janice Rule and Roddy McDowall in *The Subterraneans* (1960)

PAGE 43: The final choice for Maria, with pet (Chi Chi) and script

I T BEGAN, AS MOVIE CASTING USU-ally does, with rumors. Audrey Hepburn and Marlon Brando were two of the earliest names mentioned. George Chakiris, playing Riff (not Bernardo) in London, recalled hearing about Elizabeth Taylor and Elvis Presley. There was also some talk about the cast being made up of unknowns. A good deal of it was hearsay and publicity to drum up advance interest, and there was little discussion of anyone having an inside track. Casting *West Side Story* made for an arduous, lengthy, and inexact process. Hundreds of actors met with Robert Wise, and if the first-impression interview went well they would be asked to read audition scenes. For those who moved on, next came the screen tests. Dancers—by the hundreds—faced cattle-call auditions and performed in groups for Howard Jeffrey, Jerome Robbins's assistant. If they survived the cut, they would dance for Robbins. Seldom, in any of it, was there that life-changing millisecond when suddenly someone seemed exactly right.

Games about movie casting and "What ifs?" have long been a favorite sport for movie buffs, starting long before Scarlett O'Hara and continuing many decades later. It offers a limitless buffet of possibilities as well as some outstanding opportunities for Monday-morning quarterbacking. A few are based in historical near-misses, others are sheer wish fulfillment. With musicals there are some that are especially famous or frustrating. Cary Grant in *My Fair Lady, A Star Is Born* (1954), or even *The Music Man,* Frank Sinatra in *Carousel* (1956), Doris Day in *South Pacific*, John Travolta in *Chicago* (2002). And, in a special category, are the ones from Broadway who created the original roles and should, in the opinion of many, have done the films: Ethel Merman in *Gypsy* (1962), Julie Andrews in *My Fair Lady*, Angela Lansbury in *Mame* (1974). As for *West Side Story*, its status as a much-loved classic has not precluded after-the-fact discussion about some of its performers. Nor was Saul Chaplin's "next to impossible" assessment an exaggeration. There were thirty-five main roles, most of them with daunting requirements. Youth (or youthful appearance) was essential for all but four of them, and with a close-up Panavision 70 camera there could be no faking. For the Jets and the Sharks there needed to be dance skills acceptable to the intensely demanding Robbins. If neither Tony nor Maria had a great deal of outright dance to do, they, too, were required to move with unwonted grace, as well as project romantic appeal.

Two more requirements that might seem essential today were, in 1960, far less crucial: singing and ethnic suitability. Very few of the performers considered for the leading roles were capable of singing Bernstein's music, and those playing Puerto Rican on-screen were not required to possess any kind of Latin heritage. For many modern observers, both the dubbed voices and "Hispanic" makeup and accents may seem unsettling or

distracting. These, in the end, were two areas in which the filmmakers were content to follow traditions and practices that had been in place for many years.

The treatment of singing would forever remain one of the single biggest differences between *West Side Story* onstage and on film. For many later audience members, the result, here and in movies like *South Pacific* and *My Fair Lady*, is distancing, even disorienting: the music swells, an actor opens her or his mouth to sing, and out comes a voice that clearly belongs to someone else. In many cases, the aural perspective shifts as well, making for a total effect so artificial that it threatens to shatter whatever sense of conviction is being attempted. It can be as glaring as a film that presents the viewer with poorly done rear projection or inferior special effects. But it was an accepted element of the musical-film process from the very beginning. In *The Jazz Singer* (1927), the actors playing Al Jolson as a boy and Jolson's father moved their lips while somebody sang off camera into a microphone, much like a real-life *Singin' in the Rain*. Eventually, live singing gave way to prerecording, and from the mid-1930s on, voice doubling was an accepted part of musical filmmaking. For some actors, it was a frustrating experience—you worked hard to do your own singing and then, in the end, found that it had been replaced by something more "perfect" and, usually, less individual. Ava Gardner, for one, was incensed when her vocals for *Show Boat* (1951) were overdubbed by those of a professional.

The dubbing process was sometimes called "ghost singing," and for a good reason: the singers' names were normally kept secret, although Deborah Kerr bucked that trend by making sure that Marni Nixon got credit for her singing in *The King and I*. Sometimes dubbing was the rule, not the exception. In *South Pacific*, no one sang for themselves except Mitzi Gaynor and Ray Walston, while Pearl Bailey and Sammy Davis Jr. did their own vocals in *Porgy and Bess* and operatic voices filled in the remainder. A few of the many other beneficiaries of the process included Leslie Caron in *Gigi* (1958), Audrey Hepburn in *My Fair Lady*, and Peter O'Toole in *Man of La Mancha* (1972). In contrast, much later, the producers of *Les Misérables* (2012) made sure that everyone knew that its cast sang live on the set. Similarly, the closing credits of *Chicago* in 2002 noted specifically that its stars did all their own singing and dancing. Such things, in the time of *West Side Story*, would not have been feasible. Saul Chaplin, the man in charge of musical matters, was one of the masters at matching an on-screen face with a disembodied voice. One of his career triumphs had, after all, been *The Jolson Story*, in which Al Jolson's voice mattered far more than the actor (Larry Parks) playing him on the screen. Chaplin had signed on to *West Side Story* knowing that he was entrusted with this kind of work, and while the names of a few singers do appear in the casting notes, that particular gift—singing talent—was not the deciding factor.

With the issue of ethnicity, the filmmakers were going with conventions that had been part of film from the very beginning. It was, as Rita Moreno has said, "a very different time," and just about everyone who loves old movies has encountered odd or sometimes offensive examples, usually involving Caucasian actors playing other nationalities. One of the more infamous examples occurred in a film that opened only a few days before *West Side Story: Breakfast at Tiffany's* (1961), with Mickey Rooney as Mr. Yunioshi. Five years earlier, *The King and I* cast a wide assortment of nationalities as Southeast Asians: Swiss/Russian/Siberian (Yul Brynner); Puerto Rican (Rita Moreno, in a role originally intended for the African American Dorothy Dandridge); British (Martin Benson); Caucasian American (Terry Saunders); German-Mexican (Carlos Rivas); and, among the king's wives and children, an impressive array of nationalities spanning the entirety of Asia and well beyond.

Given all this, it is not that surprising that some of the early casting notes for *West Side Story* include such potential Marias as Nancy Kwan, born in Hong Kong, Elana Eden, from Israel, and the Italians Claudia Cardinale and Elsa Martinelli. It must be noted also that when Robert Wise began to interview prospective cast members, he (and later Robbins) did speak with a number of Hispanic actors. Among the earliest was Rita Moreno, a strong possibility for Anita from the very

OPPOSITE: Rita Moreno, the early years: a typically "fiery" role in *Untamed* (1955)

beginning, and Miriam Colon, born (like Moreno) in Puerto Rico. Susan Kohner, one of the best-known finalists for Maria, was one-half Mexican, and others under consideration for various roles included Silvia Rey, Estelita Rodriguez, and Robert Hernandez. Jose De Vega, born in California to a Filipino father and Colombian mother, had understudied the role of Chino on Broadway and would essay that role in the film, after also being in the running for Bernardo. The part–Puerto Rican Jay Norman began, in the original production, as Juano, graduated to playing Pepe and understudying Bernardo, and for the film was Pepe once again. Among the other eventual Sharks were Jaime Rogers as Loco, the Mexican-born Nick Covacevich as Toro, and Rudy Del Campo as, fittingly enough, Del Campo. (At thirty-three, Del Campo was the film's senior gang member.) Four of the Shark girlfriends were also of Hispanic descent: Yvonne Othon, Maria Jimenez, Linda Dangcil, and Olivia Perez. Besides these, the eventual Shark men and women came from backgrounds that included Russian, Greek, Turkish, European Jewish, and Japanese American.

EARLY THOUGHTS AND . . . ELVIS?

Professionally and personally, Robert Wise was not an impulsive man. His early work as a film editor required precision, care, and painstaking documentation; he took those skills with him when he became a director

and, later, a producer. Whether overseeing an enormous production, discussing financial matters with the Mirisch Company, or negotiating specifics with his codirector and screenwriter, Wise—as the surviving production correspondence makes clear—was meticulous, attentive, and perpetually mindful of detail. It would also be so when he sought to fill the roles of Tony, Maria, and all the others. His was not to be the only deciding voice, since Robbins had a major say on dance-related matters and Chaplin and the Mirisches would register their verdicts as well. Still and ultimately, he was the one giving the matter the most time and consideration. Intriguing and often surprising, Wise's casting notes for *West Side Story*—many written in his own hand—make it clear that he was determined to find the ideal Tony and Maria (in particular) and to fill all the roles with the best possible people. While some of his conclusions and decisions can be questioned, he was deliberative, wary, and usually insightful. His notes are so voluminous that, at times, they seem to comprise a casting roster of nearly every working actor of the time between the ages of about seventeen and thirty, including movie names, Broadway performers, television people, pop singers, and a few wildcards.

Most famously, there is Elvis. In the dense mythology that surrounds the name Elvis Presley, there has long been the tale that the producers of *West Side Story*, specifically Robert Wise, wanted Elvis for Tony, that possibly he was even the first choice. The

turndown came, allegedly, from Colonel Tom Parker, the singer's famously controlling manager. Parker is said to have decided it would be inappropriate for Elvis to play someone who kills his girlfriend's brother with a switchblade. Other accounts have the Colonel judging this "highbrow" production too controversial for Elvis, and also deciding that its lengthy shoot might hamper the three-films-per-year policy adopted soon after Elvis left the army in March 1960. The notion is given added piquancy, if not credence, by the fact that Elvis briefly dated both Natalie Wood and Rita Moreno years before they were cast as Maria and Anita. (Moreno wrote in her autobiography that she did so only to make her boyfriend—Marlon Brando!—jealous.) In any case, "Elvis as Tony" stories have been around as long as *West Side Story* itself and, no surprise, have been reported on the internet as historical fact.

What, then, is the truth? Could Elvis conceivably have been Wise's first choice? And, unanswerable question, how would he have made out had he played the role? While Wise himself does not appear to have commented on the subject, Elvis's name appears exactly once in Wise's notes: on an early list of ideas for Tony, apparently compiled for but not by Wise. The other names include Tony Curtis, Paul Newman, Tony Perkins, and Robert

TOP: The Tony who never was: Elvis Presley in a Tony-like moment, with Dolores Hart, in *King Creole* (1958)

BOTTOM: Anita candidate Barbara Luna in *Dime with a Halo* (1963)

Wagner—all of them older than Elvis. The list also includes a slightly more plausible group of Marias: Audrey Hepburn, Natalie Wood, Anne Bancroft, Ina Balin, Marisa Pavan, and Susan Kohner. Elvis's name was also mentioned, along with Natalie Wood's, in Army Archerd's column in *Variety* on July 22, 1959. This was less a serious report than an example of pie-in-the-sky, since it also asserted that a bunch of current pop stars, such as Fabian and Bobby Darin, were being sought to play Jets! Later, Walter Mirisch noted another unlikely possibility when he recalled "a United Artists executive who thought we should offer Tony to Harry Belafonte."

In all probability, Elvis's was one of the names thrown around in early brainstorming sessions, along with others even less conceivable, such as Taylor, Brando, and Hepburn, as well as Natalie Wood. If nothing else, leaking these names to columnists made for good publicity. Beyond that, the notion of Elvis playing Tony seems to be mostly a case of wishful thinking among Elvis fans. It does not seem likely that he was ever under serious consideration; if nothing else, his Mississippi/Memphis accent might have sounded peculiar coming out of the mouth of a New York ex-gang member. For some, hindsight may bestow a certain wistfulness, and not just among the fans, about the unrealized potential of his film career.

An Elvis or a Brando, even a Hepburn, inevitably carried a vast amount of off-screen baggage, and there would be few serious contenders for any of the roles who had anything like their prominence. Nor was there to be the opposite extreme of a Cinderella Maria or Tony appearing out of nowhere. However, Wise did go so far, at one point, to interview dozens of young women specifically because they were unknown. This occurred in April of 1960, when he had been talking with Marias, Tonys, Anitas, and the others for months. If he thought lightning might strike, it proved to not be the case, a fact which can be detected in the comments he made in his notes. They say things like "baby fat," "not for us," and "not for Maria," and Wise's sound judgment might also be deduced from the fact that not one name on the list seems, all these years later, even remotely familiar.

The question often comes up, regarding the casting, about the Broadway leads, and what reasons might there have been for them to not repeat their roles on film. The most serious possibility of all of them was the first Riff, Mickey Calin. By the time of casting, he had moved to California and entered films as Michael Callan, and was interviewed and tested for both Riff and Tony. "Lots of strength and charm," Wise noted approvingly of Callan, who had endured a stormy working relationship with Robbins during the play rehearsals. Wise also spoke to a number of other original cast members when he was in New York in February and March of 1960. While Larry Kert was apparently never under serious consideration, Wise did interview Carol Lawrence. At age

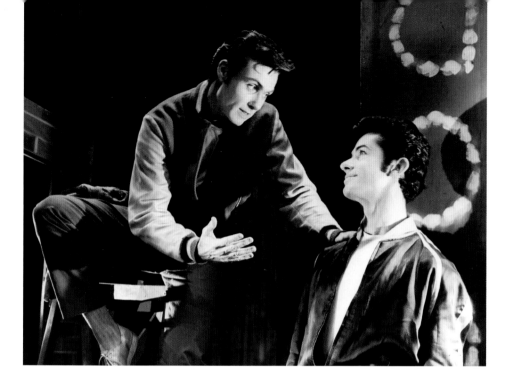

ABOVE: George Chakiris as Riff in the London company of *West Side Story*, with Don McKay as Tony

twenty-seven, she was likely felt to be on the mature side and possibly too sophisticated. Her being passed over was, she noted later, an intense disappointment. Wise also interviewed Chita Rivera, who might have been more in the running were she not already involved with a new show. *Bye Bye Birdie* was about to open, and had Rivera been at all available, Robbins would most likely have lobbied hard for her. Ken LeRoy, the first Bernardo, was by this time playing that role in London, and was tested there. For other veterans of the Broadway run being considered, prior experience with Robbins gave them an inside track. Jose De Vega, Tommy Abbott, Tony Mordente, David Winters, Tucker Smith, Larry Roquemore, Eliot Feld, Jay Norman, and brother and sister Gus and Gina Trikonis all made it into the film as Jets

and Sharks. So did Harvey Hohnecker (later Evans), a replacement Gee-Tar who was initially considered for the roles of Riff and Tony. Robbins had also cast the dancers for the London company, and several of them received the summons as well. George Chakiris, the London Riff, became the film Bernardo, while Eddie Verso (Baby John) and David Bean (Diesel) were, respectively, the film's Juano and Tiger. Ultimately, there were three members of the opening-night Broadway cast who repeated their roles on film: Abbott (Gee-Tar), Carole D'Andrea (Velma), and William Bramley (Krupke).

Most of the people Wise considered and interviewed, especially for Maria, were youngish performers with a few years' worth of credits. Few of them had a recognizable identity that might overshadow the work at

LET THEM DO WHAT THEY CAN: FINDING THE CAST

hand. One exception was Elinor Donahue, familiar to millions as Betty Anderson on the sitcom *Father Knows Best*. She showed up for her interview with Robert Wise with her dark hair dyed red—a fact which likely did little to enhance her resemblance to an ideal Maria. Wise also interviewed two former child stars attempting to sustain adult careers. Margaret O'Brien rated a "not for us" comment, while Gigi Perreau was damned with the faint praise of "nice, efficient . . . =BUT=." The most famous pair of twin sisters in show business also spoke with Wise. He had little to say about Pier Angeli, while Marisa Pavan's reading was found to be "just all right." Millie Perkins, recently in the film version of *The Diary of Anne Frank* (1959), was dismissed with a curt annotation of "no-no." A runner-up for the role of Anne Frank, Elana Eden, was judged "interesting" but "[her] quality doesn't seem ideal." Another *Anne Frank* cast member, Diane Baker, was called back for a reading that seems to have been marked by a degree of anxiety: "some lovely moments," Wise wrote, "good quality . . . tried a little hard—awfully nervous and wound up . . . will have to see." She had made a good enough impression for Wise to come back to her much later.

While some of the other hopefuls may not ultimately have been right for Maria, they did become familiar names and faces in '60s and '70s television and film: Jill St. John ("lovely but doesn't seem our Maria"), Julie Sommars, Myrna Fahey ("lovely . . . keep in mind"), Sharon Hugueny ("excellent impres-sion"), Judi Meredith, Sherry Jackson ("good possibility"), Kathleen Widdoes, Yvonne Craig, Joan Blackman. Barbara Parkins, age seventeen, did not yet have any acting credits and after reading a Maria scene was deemed "pretty good" yet "not special enough." Eighteen-year-old Yvette Mimieux drew criticism less for her blonde hair than for her gray eyes, which Wise termed, in a rare blunt comment, "VACANT." Another aspiring Maria was Victoria Vetri, who later amassed a number of credits under the name Angela Dorian and achieved greater fame as the 1968 Playboy Playmate of the Year. A certain notoriety would also accrue to another hopeful interviewed on the same day (May 25) as Vetri. Once again, Wise judged her "not for us," and indeed her prominence eventually came not with performance but through litigation. She was Michelle Triola, whose unsuccessful suit against her ex-partner Lee Marvin brought the word "palimony" into the national vocabulary. There was also an actress-dancer Wise interviewed on March 20 and found "nice—but too mature." Mary Moore had not yet begun to use her middle name of Tyler, and though the casting sheet gave her age as twenty-two she was actually a year older. She continued to work extensively in television over the next year, after which that "mature" look helped to win her the role of Laura Petrie on *The Dick Van Dyke Show*.

Some of the young men considered for Tony were actual singers. Their names, and some of the others Wise spoke with, read like the index to a 1960 fan magazine aimed at teenage girls: Ricky Nelson, who was suggested but did not audition; Troy Donahue, who interviewed with Wise on March 25; James Darren, from *Gidget,* who was one of the first actors to speak with Wise; Tommy Sands, about whom Wise commented "Good boy but questionable for us . . . dark complexion"; Frankie Avalon, who was listed as nineteen but was actually twenty ("Nice looking kid but not for us"); John Ashley ("Pretty good reading of Tony"); Ronnie Burns ("Not for us"); and, on January 28, Bobby Darin, who earned the equivocal Wise comment "Good—But?" There was also George Hamilton, whose trademark suntan was obviously in evidence even in 1960. Wise's response to him was similar to the one he had to Tommy Sands: "Too dark for us."

One potential Tony had been under consideration for the original Broadway production. At the age of twenty, Warren Beatty auditioned for the role several times and was in the running to play Riff. In May 1957, he earned a mixed response from Leonard Bernstein: "good voice—charming as hell—can't open jaw—cleancut." Less than three years later, he made an equally mixed but overall good impression on Robert Wise: "Excellent quality . . . voice not right? . . . LIKE!!" Apparently Wise continued to think of him through the entire casting process of interviews and readings. Eventually, the director viewed a test Beatty made with Natalie Wood for *Splendor in the Grass* (1961).

Along with Beatty, other Tony candidates

had major, or at very least active, careers ahead of them. Wise had little to say about Dean Jones, while the twenty-six-year-old Bert Convy was considered "Maybe little old but nice quality." Robert Drivas, who read in New York, was "a good actor but not special enough." On February 9, Wise spoke with Roy Thinnes, whose dance experience was noted, and Jack Nicholson, whose "Slow speech" was probably not an asset. The next day, Bob (Robert) Blake was rated "N.G. [no good] for us." The following week, while Wise was in New York, he wrote of Stuart Damon: "not ideal physically but a good reading and a special quality." (Damon later abandoned musical comedy for TV's *General Hospital.*) Keir Dullea, also interviewed in New York, elicited little comment, although Saul Chaplin later wrote that "he might have been chosen" had he not refused to get his longish hair cut. Dullea's fellow *2001: A Space Odyssey* (1968) astronaut, Gary Lockwood, was felt to have "not much experience," while George Segal gave what was judged a very good reading but was, again, "maybe too old." That opinion also applied to Tom Skerritt, while Mark Goddard, later of *Lost in Space* and many other TV shows, gave a "good reading—but not special enough." Richard Chamberlain, auditioning five days before his twenty-sixth birthday, was praised for his reading yet judged "TOO MATURE" in look and voice. Some of the others, many of them suggested by casting director Lynn Stalmaster, were considered but did not interview: Michael Landon,

ABOVE: Robert Redford in a 1960 television series, *Moment of Fear*

PAGES 54-55: The cast of *The Diary of Anne Frank* (1959) included two Maria hopefuls and the future Tony. From left, Shelley Winters, Lou Jacobi, Diane Baker, Ed Wynn, Joseph Schildkraut, Gusti Huber, Richard Beymer, and Millie Perkins

George Peppard, Dean Stockwell, Ben Cooper, Gary Conway, and James Franciscus.

On March 24, Wise spoke with a young actor listed on the interview sheet as Bert Reynolds, who made little impact. Neither, it seems, did a twenty-three-year-old California native—and former classmate of Natalie Wood—named Robert Redford, who interviewed with Wise the following day. Recently returned from some time doing theater work in New York, he had exactly one film/television credit to his name: a supporting role in the western series *Maverick*. The main impression he made on Wise came with his light blond hair and freckles, which might have seemed a striking contrast to the swarthy George Hamilton, also a part of that day's group of Tonys. Two weeks later, a young dancer listed as Ken Barry

[Berry] made a good impression and was called back to read the role of Tony. Wise's reaction: "good reading but too 'square' looking for us." Doug McClure, with extensive movie and TV credits that included a bit role in *South Pacific*, read several times for both Wise and Jerome Robbins. Once again, blond hair seems to have been a concern; Wise noted that McClure looked better with darker hair, but while his reading was praised he eventually fell out of the running. Wise was also impressed with a reading by Richard Davalos, who had played James Dean's brother in *East of Eden* (1955), although at twenty-nine he was considered too old. So was the former child actor Darryl Hickman, age twenty-eight.

The unavoidable feeling, while looking at these lists of names, is that on some days,

Wise's waiting room alternately resembled an episode of *Bonanza, Perry Mason,* or *The Donna Reed Show. Star Trek* and *Columbo* as well; Leonard Nimoy, interviewed on February 10, was immediately dismissed as "too old," while Peter Falk, listed as "youngish 30 character man," was surely considered only for the roles of Schrank or Krupke. Even alumni from *The Mickey Mouse Club* were considered. Doreen Tracey was quickly eliminated, Darlene Gillespie was felt to be a good possibility for Anybodys, and Bobby Burgess had the dance skills to be briefly considered for either Riff or Tony. These make it something of a surprise that, for unknown reasons, Annette Funicello was overlooked.

In many cases, the interviews and readings were not specifically for the lead roles.

While Wise spoke with many potential Jets, Sharks, Graziellas, Velmas, Anybodys, and the others, it was more crucial that Robbins and Jeffrey evaluate their dance skills. Even apart from the Broadway dancers who would be in the film, Robbins had already worked with some of them. Robert Banas, for example, had been one of the Lost Boys in Robbins's *Peter Pan* on Broadway, and was in "The Small House of Uncle Thomas" number in the *King and I* film. More recently, he had danced with Marilyn Monroe in *Let's Make Love,* as had future Shark Nick Covacevich. Both Banas and Covacevich later recalled the cattle-call nature of the dance auditions. "Hundreds of dudes," Covacevich said, "all sizes and shapes," and a winnowing-out process involving five or more follow-up calls. One possibility for Bernardo

BELOW: Before one was a Jet and the other a Shark, Robert Banas (top left) and Nick Covacevich (third from right) danced with Marilyn Monroe in *Let's Make Love* (1960).

ABOVE: The former Taffy Paul (and almost-Velma), Stefanie Powers, with former Jet Harvey Hohnecker (Evans) in her first major film, *Experiment in Terror* (1962)

had already achieved some fame at the New York City Ballet and would go on to much more. However, Edward Villella evoked drama through dance, not line readings, and Wise commented that his acting was "Not pro enough."

For the younger performers, the turndowns were often due to another manifestation of the age factor, in this case those who might be subject to the California labor laws protecting young actors from extended work hours. Thus, a fifteen-year-old New York bombshell named Joey Heatherton was interviewed and considered for the role of Graziella, then quickly eliminated. Another New Yorker, Brigid Bazlen, rated what may have been an admiring comment: "the 15 year old Liz Taylor," but, also, "too young." Similarly, on the West Coast, there was Bonnie Franklin, age sixteen, who was consid-

ered for Anybodys, Velma, and Graziella. "Dancing okay—learns fast," it was noted. The final choice for Anybodys, Susan Oakes, was also fifteen, although she turned sixteen by the time shooting began.

Another West Coast dancer, Taffy Paul, was commended for good readings for Graziella and Velma, along with the disqualifying notation of "minor . . . no." Despite her age and the resulting time restriction, she made such a good impression that she was nevertheless engaged. And therein lies a tale. Robbins had wanted Carole D'Andrea, who played Velma on Broadway, to either repeat that role on film or else be cast as Anybodys, the role she'd understudied. Unfortunately, D'Andrea had vanished and could not be located. In her absence, Taffy Paul was tapped to play Velma and began rehearsals. Then, some weeks later, D'Andrea resurfaced; she had just returned from a nine-month dance company tour of Asia sponsored by the State Department. Robbins immediately engaged her with the idea of casting her as Anybodys, and even briefly considered her for Maria. Ultimately, she returned to the role of Velma, which meant that Taffy Paul was let go. Losing the role of Velma was a disappointment, but months later, around the time she turned eighteen, Taffy Paul began amassing some performing credits. First there were a few under that name then, in a far more extensive list spanning many decades, as Stefanie Powers.

FINALLY DECIDING

When the process moved from interviews and readings to actual screen tests, six scenes were selected as the proving ground for Tony, Maria, Anita, Riff, and Bernardo. In some cases, the tests would allow the decision-makers to have a look at the actors' chemistry as well as their individual ability.

1. Bridal Shop: Maria, Tony, and Anita
2. Fire Escape: Tony and Maria
3. Apartment, after rumble: Maria and Chino
4. Doc's: Tony and Riff
5. Apartment: Maria and Bernardo
6. Doc's: Anita

Susan Kohner, a recent Oscar nominee for *Imitation of Life* (1959), tested with Rita Moreno and opposite the Tony of Scott Marlowe. Marlowe also tested with Anna Maria Alberghetti and with Michael Callan. Another Maria hopeful, a singer-dancer named Sandra Bettin, filmed scenes with Barbara Luna as Anita and Russ Tamblyn as Tony, while Ina Balin shot the fire escape scene with Corey Allen.

Wise first interviewed Rita Moreno on January 8, 1960, and she was called back numerous times to read and eventually screen-test the role of Anita. Her career by that point spanned twenty-one films, dozens of television shows and, in 1954, the cover of *Life* magazine. The range of nationalities she had played rivaled the early career of Myrna Loy; she had worn nearly every kind of "exotic" makeup and costuming. There were occasional bright spots—her sensitive Tuptim in *The King and I*, a nifty comic turn as a Marilyn Monroe type in *The Lieutenant Wore Skirts* (1956)—and, less happily, a large amount of "Latin spitfire" stereotyping. Playing Anita was far and away the best opportunity she had had in a long time. The only question came with the extent of her dance skills. Although she had trained as a child and had danced in previous films, Moreno was well aware that her skills in that area were not up to those of Chita Rivera.

One of Moreno's chief rivals for Anita was Barbara Luna, whose background encompassed Spanish, French, Portuguese, Filipino, Italian, and Hungarian. Considered for both Maria and Anita, she made several tests for the latter. Estelita Rodriguez, a Cuban-born actress and singer, had worked mainly at the terminally grade-B studio Republic, where she was often billed by her first name only. "Fine—but too old" was the judgment handed down. Officially, Rodriguez was thirty-one (in reality possibly a few years older) and one of the modest "star" vehicles she made at Republic was *The Fabulous Senorita* (1952), whose plot had her posing as Rita Moreno's twin sister. Other Anita candidates included Neile Adams, who had previously worked with Wise on *This Could Be the Night*, and Lisa Gaye, who had done, Wise noted, "much much TV." Barrie Chase, who had become famous as Fred Astaire's television dance partner, also read for Anita. The emphatic verdict, per Wise: "Not Very Good."

By June of 1960, with the start of filming weeks away, there had been countless readings, scores of callbacks, dozens of screen tests, and some final decisions. The Jets and the Sharks, male and female, were all pretty much in place, at least in theory; Robbins had not yet given some of them their specific role assignments. Meanwhile, they had started an intense round of rehearsals. Rita Moreno was all but set for Anita, the remaining question being not about her dancing but about the size of her billing. Robbins was still undecided about Bernardo, so on June 10, Wise applied some gentle pressure in a memo: "If we need Chakiris from the London company he should know immediately." George Chakiris, who had danced and appeared in bit roles in more than a dozen previous films, had left movies for the stage

two years earlier. Robbins cast him as Riff for the London production and, after about a year, he was contacted about a test. He tested (for both Riff and Bernardo) in London, along with other cast members. Later, he flew to California for more testing, opposite the Anita of Barbara Luna. By July, he was the movie Bernardo.

Wise was also nearing a final decision for the role of Tony. The leading candidates included Scott Marlowe, who had already played troubled teens in such epics as *The Cool and the Crazy* (1958) and *Young and Wild* (1958); Alan Reed Jr., whose credits included *Rock, Pretty Baby!* (1956) and *Going Steady* (1958); Corey Allen, who had appeared in both *Rebel Without a Cause* and a Republic picture titled *Juvenile Jungle* (1958); Russ Tamblyn, an Academy Award nominee in 1958 for *Peyton Place* (1957); Christopher Knight, who played the title role in *Studs Lonigan* (1960); and Richard Evans. Also, Richard Beymer, who seems to have had the inside track from his first readings (March 1960) onward. "Excellent," Wise noted, with his only reservation being about his six-feet-two-inch height. Like Tamblyn, Beymer had made the on-screen transition from adolescence to young adulthood, having most recently attracted a fair amount of "dreamboat" attention for his performance as Peter Van Daan in *The Diary of Anne Frank*. Warren Beatty was apparently still in the running, at

OPPOSITE: Russ Tamblyn in *Peyton Place* (1957), for which he received an Academy Award nomination for Best Supporting Actor

least nominally, although by May, when the tests were being made, he was on the East Coast shooting *Splendor in the Grass.*

Finally, they went with Beymer—and Tamblyn as well. After what he would recall as days spent in nerve-racking waiting, Tamblyn got a first-the-bad-news call from his agent. He'd lost Tony to the other guy, he was told, but they wanted him to play Riff. "I'll take it," he said immediately, and Mirisch contacted MGM, where Tamblyn was part of that studio's group of contract players. Absolutely not, said the studio brass. Tamblyn was already scheduled for the upcoming production of *Where the Boys Are* (1960), and the studio was not especially happy with the rougher aspects of Riff's character. Tamblyn begged and pleaded, until finally he was given the go-ahead. He had been trained as a gymnast, not a dancer, which made for some initial hostility from Robbins and Jeffrey. ("No tumbling," Robbins said at first.) Ultimately, that skill was put to good use, as it already had in two previous Tamblyn musicals, *Seven Brides for Seven Brothers* (1954) and *tom thumb* (1958).

With Maria, the indecision continued. "A fawn in the forest," someone had called Maria in an early meeting. She was not quite yet a woman, innocent, impressionable, graceful, sheltered yet capable of passion, ultimately a tragic survivor. Such a group of traits made the role more difficult to cast than the others, even setting aside singing ability. It seems that Wise may have been less aware of what he did want for the role

than observant of what, in each candidate, would not work, and all those who shot screen tests were eventually eliminated. The petite Italian soprano Anna Maria Alberghetti, who stayed in the running for a long time, was one of the few serious aspirants capable of singing the role. A familiar presence on television, she had also appeared in a few films—although, in Jerome Robbins's caustic opinion, not few enough. Scornfully referring to her as "Annamariaspaghetti," misspelling words right and left, he wrote Wise: "[Her] name is death at B.O. [box office] Mention her name and you think of a symphonic orchestra and a family of pretty dolled up Italiens singing selections from operas in a high Jeanette McDonnald vibrato."

Brooklyn native Ina Balin, who bore a marked resemblance to Carol Lawrence, gave what was felt to be an outstanding reading. Her eventual disqualification came for both vocal and physical reasons. Saul Chaplin found that Balin's breathy speaking voice made a "ludicrous" match with a double singing Maria's music in its original soprano keys. Assistant director Robert Relyea later dished on another issue: physically, she appeared too curvaceous to play a delicate seventeen-year-old. Upon seeing Balin test, Relyea recalled, Robert Wise declared, none too gracefully, "That's not a fawn . . . That's a six-point buck!" With Susan Kohner, there may have been similar issues. Her voice was distinctively nonsoprano in pitch, and she projected a sensual and robust physicality.

ABOVE: When Marias meet: finalist Susan Kohner with Natalie Wood in *All the Fine Young Cannibals* (1960)

Something similar probably held true for two actresses Wise had interviewed in New York. Both were at the beginning of major careers and both were originally held to be strong possibilities, at least until the dawn of the hard light of logic. It might be that either Suzanne Pleshette or Elizabeth Ashley could have made affecting Marias—at least until they moved from speaking in their distinctively smoky voices into a dubbed "I Feel Pretty." As for Sandra Bettin, who tested extensively, the final "no" likely came in part because, at seventeen, her age precluded full work days.

The final selection for Maria did not occur in a straightforward fashion, and does not completely tally with the story that Robert Wise would tell, with little variation, in later years. As he recalled it, neither Tony nor Maria had yet been cast, he was still considering Warren Beatty for Tony, and he borrowed Beatty's *Splendor in the Grass*

screen test from Warner Bros. "It was a test with Natalie," Wise said, "[and] the minute Natalie walked on we forgot all about [Beatty] and [said] 'There's our Maria!'" The actual timeline seems to suggest something less cut and dried than Wise's dramatic recollection. Richard Beymer was set to play Tony sometime in June of 1960, and it was after he was set for the role that he participated in the very last of the Maria screen tests. This time, the potential Maria was Diane Baker, who had read for the role earlier and who, obviously, Wise had kept in mind. She learned from her agent that Natalie Wood had already been offered the role and said no. So, for a brief time, Baker believed that she might be the choice for Maria. Then Wood changed her mind.

The name of Natalie Wood had been suggested from the very beginning, as in that 1959 *Variety* piece that also mentioned Elvis. According to Relyea, casting director Lynn

Stalmaster brought her up during an early meeting and got a response that was worse than indifference: one person threw a paper cup at him and someone else sneered, "What a tired idea. Can't you come up with someone fresh and exciting?" Fresh or exciting were, of course, subjective concepts; what is less disputable is that, except for Audrey Hepburn or the even less likely Elizabeth Taylor, Wood was the single best-known candidate for Maria. She was so familiar, in fact, that by 1960 she was being taken for granted, having seldom been out of public view for well over a decade.

Wood had begun acting at the age of five, and by nine had appeared prominently in a bona fide classic, *Miracle on 34th Street* (1947). From childhood to adolescence and on to adulthood, she was seldom absent on either movie or television screens. She had played the daughter of Bette Davis, Jimmy Stewart, and Bing Crosby, the niece of John Wayne, and (on TV) the sweetheart of Tom Sawyer. She had costarred in a forgotten sitcom called *The Pride of the Family* and donned a blonde wig to play Virginia Mayo as a girl in *The Silver Chalice* (1954). At seventeen, she was nominated for an Academy Award for her breakthrough role in *Rebel Without a Cause*, but there was little in the way of exciting follow-up. As a contract player at Warner Bros., she was relegated mainly to routine fare with few opportunities. *Marjorie Morningstar* (1958), adapted from a best-selling novel, turned out disappointingly, and films like *Bombers B-52* (1957) and *The Girl He Left*

Behind (1956) did little more than keep her name before the public. The primary attention she seemed to draw was off-screen—a succession of high-profile dates and, finally, marriage to actor Robert Wagner. From a professional point of view, Wood's stardom was, by 1960, more a matter of celebrity than achievement, and she was actively seeking better opportunities. She finally got one with *Splendor in the Grass*, directed by Elia Kazan and shot in New York in the spring and summer of 1960.

Wood was still filming *Splendor* when she was contacted yet again about *West Side Story*. Wise and Robbins were in New York as well, preparing to do the location filming. Bowing to the perquisites of stardom, the codirectors took a fast trip down to Atlantic City, where Wood and Wagner had gone for a performance by Frank Sinatra. Wise and Robbins made the offer again, and this time she accepted. At a hefty $250,000, her salary would be double what she had been offered originally. Presented with the option of a lower fee plus a percentage, she chose to take the flat sum.

As soon as she finished work on *Splendor in the Grass*, Wood immediately began to prepare. Even for a large-scale blockbuster, the new film presented her with a formidable list of challenges. There would be dance rehearsals, wardrobe fittings, hair and makeup tests, and working on a convincing Puerto Rican accent. Also, crucially, voice training. Determined to do her own singing on-screen, she began long and sometimes grueling sessions with vocal coach Bobby Tucker. While she had not to that point sung in films, she had done so on television. In a 1958 duet with Sinatra on "Them There Eyes," her voice rings out with some authority and, even opposite Sinatra, she manages to hold up her end of the song. Given Wood's career drive, it's no surprise that she wanted to do Maria's songs. Whether or not Saul Chaplin ever believed she could is another matter.

With Wood's engagement, the cast was virtually complete. One role remained uncast, and was not to be filled until shooting in Hollywood was well underway. This was the small but conspicuous part of Glad Hand, the clueless social worker who leads the dance at the gym. On November 2, Wise heard readings by three actors, all of them familiar (or soon to be) on television. Hal Smith, the town drunk Otis on *The Andy Griffith Show,* gave an "obvious" reading, while Joe Flynn (*McHale's Navy* and scores of others) was "excellent." The ultimate victor, however, was judged "wonderful": John Astin, the future Gomez on *The Addams Family.*

From the first trial balloons to that one last role, the casting had taken well over a year. At no point had either Wise or Robbins been in any way half-hearted or expedient. They wanted the finest possible cast, and at the end of it, there was little sense that they had compromised or settled. There was a superb group of dancers, and the experienced group of leads included one authentically starry movie name. Assembling this

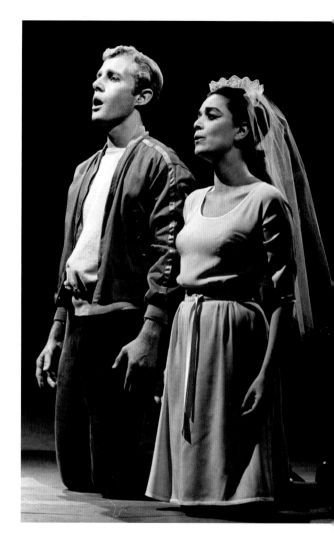

ABOVE: A Maria film hopeful who eventually played the role onstage: Anna Maria Alberghetti, with Lester James, in a 1965 production of *West Side Story* at the Melody Top Theatre in Milwaukee

cast had taken longer than originally anticipated. So, as was soon clear, would the filming.

CHAPTER FOUR

HALFWAY THERE: FROM HOLLYWOOD TO NEW YORK

"Robbins wanted perfection at any cost, so we did many, many, many takes."

ROBERT BANAS
(Joyboy)

ABOVE: Eleven years before *West Side Story* took to the streets of Manhattan, *On the Town* gave filmgoers a quick tour of some of the city's neighborhoods. Here, as part of the "New York, New York" sequence, Jules Munshin, Frank Sinatra, and Gene Kelly explore Chinatown.

PAGE 66: Leaving the 110th Street playground in high-flying style: Eliot Feld, Tucker Smith, Tony Mordente, Tommy Abbott, Russ Tamblyn

BEFORE THE SECOND WORLD War, very few of the many films set in New York City were actually shot there. They would use second unit or stock footage of Times Square, the Empire State Building, the Brooklyn Bridge, and the like, while the actors themselves seldom left California. In the postwar era, filmmakers soon realized that authentic locations made movies candid and vibrant in ways they had not been before. The crime drama *The Naked City* (1948) was vivid testament to the fact that nothing in California could ever duplicate real New York streets, and MGM's *On the Town* took the audacious step of venturing outside studio walls to stage some of its musical sequences in and around the city's actual landmarks. Later, Marilyn Monroe stopped traffic when she stood on a subway grate near the corner of Lexington Avenue and East 52nd Street while shooting *The Seven Year Itch* (1955). That film, like many others, made use of both locations and studio soundstages. That was also going to be the approach taken with *West Side Story*. Robert Wise wanted New York realism, and Jerome Robbins preferred a less literal studio look. In a way, they both won.

The film could not and would not be shot entirely on location. The logistics were next to impossible and the cost astronomical. Thus, in its shooting schedule as well as in the result on-screen, *West Side Story* began in Manhattan and finished in Hollywood. Wise had already shown his affinity for urban locations with *Somebody Up There Likes Me* and *Odds Against Tomorrow*, and the Mirisch Company and United Artists felt that his was the right way to get the movie started. The Prologue—Robbins's thrilling onstage scene-setter—was to be shot in New York locations, as would the first scene with the police and portions of "Jet Song." Then the company would return to the Goldwyn studio for the remainder. The first question came with what locations to use, and in several trips from late 1959 through mid-1960, Wise traveled to New York to get ideas. Along with a small production team and sometimes Robbins, he visited different neighborhoods, took photos, and strategized. Nothing of this sort had ever been attempted before, not even in *On the Town*, and snapshots survive, in Wise's archives, showing the kind of look and feel they had in mind: ruined tenements, decaying facades, depressed cityscapes, various bleak urban details. Eventually, Robbins directed a few dancers using 16mm test film to get an idea of how his choreography might play on a real street. A *New Yorker* reporter watched some of the test shoot, as did a crew from the city's Department of Sanitation. Informed that this dilapidated site was going to be a movie set, one of the sanitation workers reacted with disdain: "When you think of all the nice places to make a movie in New York, and they pick this!"

As might be expected, much of the direc-tors' focus fell on the "real" site of *West Side Story*, the area in which the play had been set. As it happened, this was a fateful moment for that neighborhood, which was officially known as Lincoln Square and sometimes called San Juan Hill. Encompassing roughly twenty blocks, it was situated in Manhattan's West 60s, bordered on the east by Columbus Avenue and the west by the Hudson River. In the late nineteenth and early twentieth centuries, it had been a thriving area, a predominantly African American center for culture and activity densely packed with tenement apartments, warehouses, and other businesses. This began to change after World War II, when a major change in demographics saw many of its residents moving uptown to Harlem. They were replaced by thousands of families newly arrived from Puerto Rico. Gang violence, often an element of the neighborhood, began to escalate considerably, and Amsterdam Avenue served as the dividing line between factions. The Puerto Rican residents lived west of Amsterdam, the descendants of European immigrants were on the east; the skirmishes between these rival gangs had provided the basis for *West Side Story*.

By the late 1950s, the formerly vibrant neighborhood was in worse shape than ever, which made it an inevitable target for New York's ultra-powerful "Master Builder," Robert Moses. As head of the Mayor's Committee on Slum Clearance (one of many titles he bore), Moses invoked the power of eminent domain to seize the area and, in effect, obliterate it. In 1959 and 1960, the area's residents, around

seven thousand families and eight hundred businesses, were ordered to pack up and vacate. Although they were promised financial assistance, few of them received any kind of compensation. Mostly they moved to Harlem and the Bronx, and their former homes and businesses were torn down to make way for high-rise apartment units and, most conspicuously, the performing arts complex to be known as Lincoln Center.

The demolition of Lincoln Square was already underway by the time Wise began his search for locations, and his snapshots show a number of blocks completely leveled, with only rubble to indicate where the "actual" Sharks and Jets had lived and fought. One area where the wrecking ball had not yet made too damaging a mark was the 200 block of West 68th Street, between West End and Amsterdam Avenues, two blocks northwest of the upper border of the Lincoln Center site. As with most of Lincoln Square, it was crowded with tenements and businesses. While demolition had begun on many of the buildings themselves, their facades were relatively intact—some of them like movie sets

TOP: Some Jets aloft in front of the St. Matthew's Rectory. From left, Tucker Smith, Bert Michaels, Anthony Teague, Robert Banas, David Bean (rear), and Harvey Hohnecker.

BOTTOM: Sharks vs. Jets at the playground on East 110th Street. From left, Gus Trikonis, Eddie Verso, George Chakiris, Jay Norman, Jaime Rogers, Eliot Feld, and Tony Mordente.

PAGES 72–73: Looking east on West 68th Street, with a view of the Royal Garage. George Chakiris, Eliot Feld, Tucker Smith, Russ Tamblyn, David Winters, and (at rear) Harvey Hohnecker.

with nothing in back of them. Among the structures still extant, in some form, in the summer of 1960:

- Public School No. 94, located at 201 West 68th Street.

- The former Domino Fuel Corporation at 210 West 68th Street. For *West Side Story*, it was outfitted with a "new" facade that renamed it the Spano Travel Agency and gave it the incorrect street number of 180.

- St. Matthew's Rectory, 216 West 68th Street. The Church of St. Matthew, one block south, was already demolished.

- The Royal Garage, 222 West 68th Street, whose large sign is apparent in a number of shots.

- The Endicott Express warehouse, 241 West 68th Street.

The one block west of this one, past West End Avenue, was almost completely leveled, and would serve as the site of the pile of rubble where the Sharks threw vegetables at the Jets. Beyond that was the West Side Elevated Highway and then the Hudson River. Wise later recalled making a deal with the contractor, one Phil Ursaner of the Eagle Demolition Co., paying "five or ten thousand dollars" to work elsewhere in the area and save this street for last. Without the intervention of the movie people, the block would have been gone by the time filming started in the second week of August.

With the enhancements of some additional signs and windows and general spruce-up by production designer Boris Leven, that one doomed block of West 68th Street briefly regained a hint of its former patina and, ultimately, a kind of poignant immortality. With careful camera angles and editing, the filmmakers were able to turn it into something resembling an active city street, albeit one in decline. Then, following this stay of execution, it would all be gone. The buildings were taken down, as planned, and then the street itself was physically erased off the Manhattan map. The spot where that section of West 68th Street once ran was promptly taken up, in large part, by a section of Lincoln Towers, a complex of six 28- and 29-story buildings. Lincoln Towers is composed mainly of apartments, which began as rentals and then, in 1987, became condos. In 2015, they were joined by a 21-story building known as 170 Amsterdam Apartments at the far east end of the former street. That structure stands over the precise point where West 68th Street once began to go westward past Amsterdam Avenue. The complex, which also includes parking areas and small patches of grass, contains nothing to give any hint that it was once a busy street. Robert Moses had done his job thoroughly.

The other primary location for the shoot was the playground, which included a basketball court. It was nowhere near West 68th Street, nor part of the Lincoln Square neighborhood, nor even on the West Side. Wise's goal had been appearance, not location, and the playground that ultimately fit the bill was (and remains) on East 110th Street between

Third and Second Avenues, directly behind P.S. 83. (East 110th is now known as Tito Puente Way, and P.S. 83 is now called the Luis Munoz Rivera School.) Movie editing often laughs at geography, and the shots in the Prologue that cut deftly between the playground and the street are, in reality, spanning a walking or driving distance of about four miles. For the later scenes set there, the playground was reproduced in smaller form on a Hollywood soundstage.

The third component of the New York shoot was also the first scene to be shot. It is, in effect, the prologue to the Prologue. During the final notes of the overture, the abstract lines on the screen dissolve into the contours of Manhattan's skyline, pre–World Trade Center, in an aerial view looking north from New York Harbor. Cut to a series of straight-down overhead shots that take in much of the island: the George Washington and Triborough (now Robert F. Kennedy) bridges, a dock on the West Side, Battery Park, Wall Street, Rockefeller Center, the United Nations, the Empire State Building, the old Yankee Stadium. "A kind of abstract New York," Wise said, regarding his intention. "The New York that even New Yorkers hadn't seen." While such sequences are usually the work of a second-unit crew, Wise took a hands-on approach to choosing the shots. During his last preliminary trip to New York, he engaged a helicopter and went up with assistant director Relyea. With its side door removed, the copter began prowling above Manhattan to give Wise some ideas. Then came the fun part, as Relyea

remembered: "I held his belt and he hung out of the helicopter. I literally had one hand on the door overhead and my right hand holding Bob's belt and let him dangle out there until he finally said, 'I've got it.'"

The actual filming, a month later, was done with more safety precautions in place, as well as a large Panavision 70 camera. From a distance of six decades, Wise's hazardously conceived montage may seem a predictable call to make for a film set in Manhattan. At the time, it was a sensation, all the more so for its soundtrack: a low rumble of urban sound punctuated by gang whistles and bongo drums. It was also, however unintentionally, an homage to the first real movie musical, *The Broadway Melody*. That, too, had opened with a succession of aerial shots of Manhattan—a cinematic flourish that worked in early 1929 and did so again here, late in 1961.

Originally, and quite optimistically, the New York shoot was to have covered far more territory and included more cast members. There were going to be shots of Tony and Maria, as well as a far greater number of locations that included a back alley running between West 24th and 25th Streets, a slaughterhouse on West 41st, a swimming pool on

OPPOSITE: It was still chilly in New York when Jerome Robbins (left) and Robert Wise (right) photographed a possible *West Side* location with the aid of three prospective "Jet Girls," including Gina Trikonis (next to Robbins).

PAGES 76-77: Dancers need to warm up, even on location, even on West 68th Street. Tony Mordente, Anthony Teague, Tommy Abbott, David Winters, Nick Covacevich, Eddie Verso, Tucker Smith, Eliot Feld, Harvey Hohnecker, and Jay Norman at the barre.

West 59th, a handball court at 126th and Amsterdam, a housing project on East 106th, and several warehouses, street views, and walls. In the end, there was no time to photograph any of these. As it was—and without Tony and Maria—the shooting went far over the original sixteen work days that had been planned for it.

For more than two months prior to the start of the Manhattan shoot, Robbins had been in California rehearsing his Jets and Sharks, which eventually included Tamblyn and Chakiris. Each morning, assistant Howard Jeffrey took the dancers through warm-ups, after which Robbins stepped in to work on the actual choreography. With typical rigor and occasional obsessiveness, he drilled and pushed and criticized and

created. Punctuating his drive for perfection was a motto he repeated frequently: "Once it's on film it's there forever." As in the stage rehearsals, he encouraged competition and segregation, even animosity, between the two gang groups, correctly believing that this gave the dancing heightened vigor and conviction. On film, as on the stage, the characterizations of the Jets were delineated far more fully than those of the Sharks. They had more stage (and then screen) time, as well as better defined motivations. Such was the way Laurents and Robbins had shaped the material originally, without deliberate bias but with, inevitably, a kind of slant.

Another kind of divide existing between many of the dancers was due not to country of origin but to professional background. It

BELOW: The Robbins approach: the codirector gives some dance direction to Jay Norman, George Chakiris, and Eddie Verso on West 68th Street.

was, in essence, a case of Broadway vs. Hollywood. A number of Jets and Sharks had already worked with Robbins on the original show. They knew the moves, the music, and the characters, and they knew how Robbins worked. Others, Tamblyn included, were California-based film veterans, not versed in the Robbins style but familiar with the intricate peculiarities involved in dancing in front of the camera. (Robert Banas, for his part, had done both, including working with Robbins on stage and on film.) Each group had something the other needed, and sometimes the Broadway people could be, as Jet David Winters termed it, "artistic snobs" toward both the dancers with film experience and the movie actors cast in lead roles. Eventually the rivalry gave way to a kind of mutual understanding and rapport. They were, after all, in it together.

To the uninitiated it soon became obvious that Robbins's genius came at a high price. The New Yorkers, having already worked under him, accepted and even thrived under his hard-edged leadership style. "We were," Harvey Hohnecker [Evans] said much later, "used to dictators." Any kind of pain being

TOP: Jerome Robbins and crew on West 68th Street

BOTTOM: Jerome Robbins leads a group of dancers during the lengthy audition process.

PAGES 80–81: Jerome Robbins and some of his Sharks and Jets are all smiles as they take a break from rehearsal to stroll down the main street of the Goldwyn lot. From left: Rita Hyde, Jay Norman, George Chakiris, Yvonne Othon, Tony Mordente, rehearsal pianist Betty Walberg, Eddie Verso, David Bean, Tommy Abbott, and Robbins.

inflicted, physical or psychological, came with the territory. Comments by the dancers reveal the double edge. David Winters: "Definitely a sadist . . . but I love him"; Tony Mordente: "You work with Jerry Robbins, and you're a slave"; Yvonne Othon: "If you didn't get it the way he wanted, he could be pretty mean"; Carole D'Andrea: "I knew never, never to show him any fear." Gina Trikonis: "His eyes [would get] that look— that red, wide-eyed, glazed, non-blinking, lethal, all-hell-is-about-to-break-loose look"; David Bean: "If you worked hard for him, he absolutely adored you. If you showed signs of slacking off a bit, he'd kill you."

For those without prior exposure to Robbins, it was a different story. Saul Chaplin, who observed the dance rehearsals with a kind of horrified fascination, found the atmosphere in the rehearsal hall to be so fraught that it resembled, in his charged phrase, "a concentration camp."

They didn't dance out of joy, they danced out of fear. His reputation for being difficult had preceded him, but this was much worse than I had expected. I wondered how he ever got anyone to work for him until I asked one of the dancers. The reply was "How else would I ever get a chance to dance like that?" I didn't invent the notion, but it's further proof that being a successful dancer requires a certain degree of masochism.

TOP: Robert Wise crouches in one of the holes dug into West 68th Street. Meanwhile, Jerome Robbins tries some moves while, at rear, Jay Norman, George Chakiris, and Eddie Verso wait their turn.

BOTTOM: Robbins tries out one of the seesaws at the playground on East 110th Street.

Perhaps the divergence of opinion over Robbins is best illustrated by an exchange Russ Tamblyn and George Chakiris had in a 2011 interview:

Tamblyn: There is a book about him called *Dance with Demons*. Hello! Hello! Do you get the picture? I've done two tributes to him, and everyone says the same thing, he was a f**king pain in the ass.
Chakiris: I've read the book as well, but they still all say they would work with him at the drop of a hat. I loved Jerry. You rose to another level because of him.

With some of the dancers, Robbins observed their work and personalities during weeks of rehearsals before he gave them their specific assignments. There were some surprises and shuffling, as some of the Broadway veterans found that they were not to be cast in their original roles. Tony Mordente, A-Rab on the stage, was made Action, while David Winters, Broadway's Baby John, would be A-Rab. The movie's Baby John, Eliot Feld, had replaced Winters on Broadway. Jay Norman moved from Juano to Pepe, while Harvey Hohnecker, a replacement Gee-Tar, was now Mouthpiece. Larry Roquemore, also a replacement Gee-Tar, was moved to the other side as the Shark Rocco, while Tucker Smith, a stage replacement for both Riff and Diesel, was put in as the new Jet, Ice. All three members from the London cast—Chakiris, Eddie Verso, and David Bean—all found themselves in different roles as well. The changes ultimately had a positive effect: confronted with new characters, the dancers were compelled to rethink and freshen their approach. Since Robbins based his choreography as much on characterization as on movement, this paid constant dividends throughout the shoot and in the finished film, "Cool," in particular, would be possibly the most exciting and intense number in the film for this reason, and for the dancers the most grueling.

Another part of the Robbins technique involved giving the dancers multiple variations on the same theme. His imagination was such that he could come up with any number of different ways to stage or dance a given passage, and the troupe was expected to learn them all and be ready to do any of them on demand. Bert Michaels (Snowboy) counted nineteen versions of the moment when Bernardo intercepts the basketball. "We all did one version after another by rote until he was satisfied and we were numb. He finally settled on one, which was comprised of several sections of each of the variations we had rehearsed. Then he said, 'That's it!'"

The company had already been rehearsing for some weeks when Robbins spoke to the *New York Times.* "I want the movements sharp," he said of the Prologue, "like a pistol shot." Sharp, but also scaled down for the camera. "We have to bring the dancers in to get the maximum impact. We're not trying to reach the last row of the balcony, but that camera in front row center." The reporter also discussed numbers with Robbins: "Since May, Mr. Robbins has auditioned over 2,000 dancers, male and female, for some forty openings. Thus far, twelve dancers with 'West Side Story' stage experience have been signed, but none of the original leads is among them. They are already too old, Mr. Robbins feels. The average age of the dancers in the film will be about twenty-one, but some are only seventeen."

A few were even younger. Although Eliot Feld turned eighteen two days after the article ran, Susan Oakes, cast as Anybodys, was barely sixteen. Evidently the youngest of all the dancers was a fourteen-year-old named Elaine Joyce. Cast as Hotsie, Tiger's girlfriend, she can be spotted, intermittently, in the gym sequence. She was far more in evidence in later years when she starred on Broadway in the musical *Sugar*, appeared on innumerable 1970s TV game shows, and became the wife of Neil Simon.

Robbins used some of the rehearsal time to work out some further ideas about the Prologue. Having already done some test shooting at the prospective Manhattan location, he decided to try some more in California, with quite memorable results. Along with Robbins, Relyea, a reduced film crew, and assorted personnel, Tamblyn and a group of Jets were transported from the Goldwyn studio to a rundown section of downtown Los Angeles. There, on a genuine and active street, with locals watching from the sidelines and rehearsal pianist Betty Walberg playing on the back of a truck, they began to dance the Prologue. The reaction from onlookers was first stunned silence, then open hostility. "As any riot does," Relyea recalled, "it just broke out. I mean, things

started to fly, and here they came. And we headed for the cars, and there were people hanging on the back of the cars as we pulled away." Months later, when it was necessary to go back to the streets of Los Angeles for a few shots in the "Tonight Quintet," they managed to find a suitable yet peaceful location in another part of town.

During the entire rehearsal period, it had become apparent that the Jets and the Sharks were out of their teen years (for the most part) only in a technical sense. When not actually dancing, they tended to act up, and act out, like an especially unruly pack of adolescents. When things moved from rehearsal to actual filming, the situation intensified accordingly. While energy is an essential requirement for dancers, these young men (and some of the women) coupled natural exuberance with a sizable affinity for mischief. As dancers and actors, they followed directions and did as they were told, but when not engaged in this fashion, things could go haywire. Relyea was entrusted with watching and, more often than not, reprimanding a group of Jets and Sharks that he later described as "twenty wild animals." "I think I did yell 'QUIET' eight, nine thousand times," he said, and his workspace became known as "the principal's office." It was not at all uncommon to see a group of miscreants lined up, waiting to receive one of his lectures. Cast members liked to compare him to Officer Krupke, and usually he was about that effective in curbing their misbehavior. One stunt they

ABOVE: Riff and the Jets, ready for their New York adventure: Tommy Abbott, Eliot Feld, David Winters, Tucker Smith, Russ Tamblyn, Anthony "Scooter" Teague, Tony Mordente, Harvey Hohnecker, Bert Michaels, David L. Bean, and Robert Banas.

PAGES 84-85: Shooting the Jets on West 68th Street. Jerome Robbins and cinematographer Daniel Fapp stand by the camera. Production photographer Ernst Haas is on the ladder at left.

devised became an ongoing ritual, especially during birthday celebrations: forcibly holding down members of the cast or crew to shave their crotches. "The casualty list for that prank," Relyea said, "was substantial, judging by the number of people walking around the set furiously scratching themselves." It might be noted that what seemed like rowdy horseplay at that time appears to wear a more hostile face many years later.

In early August 1960, the Jets and Sharks flew to New York for the location shoot. As soon as they arrived at the Warwick Hotel in Manhattan, they were kept on as short a leash as possible. Along with Tamblyn and Chakiris, the location-shoot contingent

numbered those "twenty wild animals," directors Wise and Robbins, Relyea, director of photography Daniel Fapp, a schoolteacher for those still underage, and more than two dozen others, plus a large amount of equipment and vehicles. The weather in Manhattan in that summer of 1960 was not unbearably hot, at least for the average person. "Average," however, does not begin to describe what the cast members were doing. Their work started on August 10, after Wise and the crew had seen to the majority of the opening aerial shots. Under a bright sun, plus additional lights and reflectors, they went through Robbins's exacting choreography again and again while the 70mm Pana-

vision camera shot them from eye level, from up high on a crane, or, most arrestingly, from a low angle created by placing the camera into holes deeply dug into West 68th Street.

On most days the cast would get dressed and made up at the Warwick, then get in buses that took them to West 68th or East 110th Streets. Often, Robbins demanded that they arrive early for warm-up barre exercises on the sidewalk, a ritual which made them feel especially self-conscious. This came, in part, because they were being watched. As home movies taken by Jets Harvey Hohnecker and Robert Banas show, sizable crowds gathered, behind police barricades, to observe the filming. It quickly became obvious that the onlookers included real-life gang members from the neighborhood, which did not add to anyone's feeling of security. At one point, word went around that a stabbing had occurred not far from the set, and though no film people were involved, it was clear that additional protection might not be a bad thing. The solution, as recalled by Relyea and several Jets, involved hiring several locals, mostly gang members, to provide a firm and reassuring "security" presence during the shoot. Presumably, they did their job well enough for no further incidents, stabbings or otherwise, to have been reported. Nevertheless, it was observed at one point that a camera was dented by a flying brick.

For Robbins, positioned alongside Wise near the camera, safety may have been less of an issue than artistic truth. Still con-cerned about the clash between stylized dance and genuine settings, he devised the solution of having Tamblyn and the Jets begin the Prologue by simply walking. Almost undetectably, the walking would grow more rhythmic, with small gestures and moves, first from one or two of the Jets, then more. At first they seemed like nervous manifestations of character, then grew and continued until it became, in effect, the outright dance of the original show. It was the perfect bridge between the two poles, and Robbins made them do it for take after take after take, all the while repeating "Once it's on film it's there forever." While his temper was under reasonable control, the drive for perfection continued and even increased. Tamblyn recalled shooting one especially long scene on a stretch of West 68th Street in which he and the other Jets got through the intricate and exacting choreography without any apparent slip-ups, and Wise declared himself satisfied. Not so Robbins, who demanded that they go back and do the entire thing again starting on the other foot—which necessitated more rehearsal and a think-fast-on-your-feet transposition of all the gestures and steps they had just done.

Accustomed to the free creative rein he had on the stage and in rehearsals, Robbins showed little desire to alter his style when cameras were present. Sometimes, after approving a take, he would suddenly decide that he needed further "coverage" and shoot the action from another angle. This meant a complete stop, then unplanned time spent in repositioning the camera for another shot and another group of takes. The cost, in money as well as time, soared, and the performers were frequently pushed near a breaking point. On one especially hot day at the 110th Street playground, Tony Mordente and Jaime Rogers were required to do their fight scene repeatedly. When Mordente requested a quick break from the strenuous work and blazing temperatures, Robbins refused and ordered him to stay where he was. More and more takes followed. For the sequence of Baby John being chased by the Sharks, Robbins demanded so many takes that Eliot Feld stopped, upon hearing "Cut" and began to vomit. Then, as Robbins's assistant Margaret Banks recalled, "Jerry would say, 'Sorry, Eliot, we've got to do it again. We didn't get it.'"

The Manhattan shoot had originally been scheduled to last three weeks. It ended up running about six, well into September. The amount of usable footage shot per day averaged out to approximately half a minute of screen time—an extremely low amount that seemed lower still to those paying attention to the cash flow. Some of the delay came from that traditional curse on location shooting: uncooperative weather. For this a number of the dancers took at least partial credit. On one particularly warm day, they decided enough was enough, and they would combine their artistic gifts with their bent for playful havoc. With David Winters and Tony Mordente taking the lead, the dancers

formed a circle and began an impromptu version of a Native American rain dance. It proved to be surprisingly effective, and as the drops began to fall shooting was suspended for the rest of the day. After rain canceled several more days of work, a handwritten note from Robert Wise was posted in the makeup room: NO MORE RAIN DANCES!

As sensible as the codirector setup seemed on paper, it was far less practical in application. These two men, with their wildly disparate backgrounds and personalities, had differing goals, concepts, and priorities. Wise, as producer, was conscious of the time and money spent and usually attempted to move on to the next shot, while Robbins was always sensing the possibility of getting the last shot to be *even better*. As Rita Moreno put it, "The hardest time he had in the world, in this film, was to say 'Print it. That's the perfect take.' Because [for him] there was no perfect take." While the clock ticked and the cast and crew waited, Robbins thought and rethought every shot while also spending a significant amount of time in deliberations with Wise. These discussions, it was observed, could become discordant. Much that was shot turned out to be unused and sometimes unusable, and the time element made it necessary to scrap plans to shoot at the other New York locations that had been selected. While the filming continued its slow and delay-ridden course, the timeless and unending conflict between Art and Business played out, in all its complexity, right there on the New York streets.

Ultimately, the product of all this effort and aggravation spoke for itself. Once assembled from all the pieces shot on those two locations four miles apart, the Prologue was magnificent. So were Wise's aerial shots and the open-air staging of "Jet Song." For many viewers, these opening eighteen minutes would be the highlight of the film. Robbins's concept and Wise's experience had joined, however arduously, to create something brilliant. Now there remained the entire rest of the film to shoot. As the company returned to California in September, those responsible for the budget and schedule were beginning to wonder—as film people often do—if the art might continue to justify the cost.

TOP: The heat was intense and the paint was real. The Sharks let the Jets have it, just off West 68th Street.

BOTTOM: Robert Wise appears to be demonstrating a dance move in the middle of West 68th Street for Jerome Robbins, George Chakiris, and Eddie Verso.

OPPOSITE: Jets all the way, on East 110th Street: (clockwise from lower left) David Winters, Robert Banas, Tucker Smith, Anthony Teague, David Bean, Tommy Abbott, and Bert Michaels.

CHAPTER FIVE
FAIR FIGHT: THE HOLLYWOOD CHRONICLES

—

"How did they ever think we could catch up when it took as long as it did just to film the 'Prologue'?"

TONY MORDENTE
(Action)

ABOVE: Natalie Wood working on her songs with vocal coach Bobby Tucker

PAGE 91: Rita Moreno launches into "America." At rear, from left, Maria Jimenez, Jaime Rogers, Yvonne Othon, Olivia Perez, and Andre Tayir

THINGS WERE NOT IDLE ON THE West Coast during the New York shoot. The Goldwyn lot was filling up with large sets in various stages of completion, the costumes were being finished and, beginning on August 22, the newly cast Maria was testing her hair, makeup, and costumes, as well as working on her dancing, singing, and Puerto Rican accent. Although Natalie Wood was a latecomer to the production, the delays in New York gave her more preparation time, besides which she would not be part of the first scenes shot in Hollywood. In Robbins's and Jeffrey's absence, she and Rita Moreno and the other women worked on their numbers under the supervision of Yvonne Othon, deputized to serve as dance captain. Walter and

Harold Mirisch had also remained in California, closely observing the escalating tallies of days and dollars. Aware of the quality of the work being created, they were also seeking to placate United Artists and the money people. The hope was that Wise and Robbins, once back in California, could make up for the time and expense that had been lost in Manhattan. It was, at the very least, a goal, and with an extraordinary swiftness that would never characterize the speed of filming, it proved to not be the case.

After the company returned from New York in the second week of September, the early work in the studio centered around "America," filmed on Stage 5. Beginning on day one, it was clear that only one thing had changed from the location work: weather was not going to be a factor. Most days consisted of a final rehearsal on the set, with many corrections and much fine-tuning from Robbins, after which Wise would call "Speed" and the camera rolled. Then, at the end of the shot, "Cut." Unless an actor had made a mistake, or if some urgent point had been slighted, Wise was generally satisfied. Then, from Robbins, "Do it again," and they did. Fourteen takes, twenty takes, and more. "Geez Jerry," Wise would plead, "it looked good to me." Then followed another one. The daily shooting records quickly began to tell a story of repeated takes of most individual shots, long rehearsal times, and per-day totals of usable footage that seemed, to those watching the budget, far less than acceptable.

As work got underway, Harold Mirisch sent the two directors a memo emphasizing the most salient points:

The New York film is most exciting and we're all very pleased with it. It's too bad it had to cost so much but that's the gamble with location filming.

However, now that the New York shooting is completed and you're back in the safety of the studio, you must pick up the pace of the shooting so the picture doesn't get impossibly behind schedule and over budget.

One way you can help cost-wise is to cut down on the number of takes you make on each set-up. As you know, this 70 mm film is fantastically expensive and as a result of your very extensive coverage in New York, we are far over our film budget to this point. Please do not start filming a set-up . . . until it is really ready so you'll have a chance to "get it" in the first couple of takes. . . .

Do keep strongly in mind the importance of holding the picture within a budget that we can manage.

As if to show the memo's effectiveness, the next day's total was two shots that required twenty-eight takes, plus several hours of rehearsal. Thus, in those first few days, it became plain to the Mirisches that Relyea's original estimate of a ten-week studio shoot had been optimistic to the point of delusion. By September 15, Harold Mirisch was reiterating to Wise and Robbins that "These items [long rehearsals and multiple takes] add up to many, many hundreds of thousands of dollars and I think we must make it a policy to cut down the time of rehearsals and also the number of takes." Then came the veiled warning: "If we do not finish this sequence by Friday, I would like to meet with both of you to discuss the modus operandi from here on in."

By beginning with "America," the company was doing some formidable frontloading. The number had been completely reconceived to include men as well as women and Sondheim had written new lyrics, making it essentially a new piece. Certainly Robbins approached it that way. He had not choreographed the number on Broadway, instead delegating the work to Peter Gennaro. For the movie, Robbins staged the men's movements while the women's choreography remained basically what Gennaro had already done, with Broadway veterans Carole D'Andrea and Gina Trikonis enlisted to coach Rita Moreno and the other women in the Gennaro moves. Robbins, D'Andrea observed, was especially hard on Moreno, for the simple reason that "She wasn't Chita."

At one point, early in "America," Robbins

demanded a change that went well beyond arranging the dances or directing the cast. The dancers recall him taking a long look at the rooftop set and then remarking, "The wall doesn't work." Full stop for some reconfiguration to what, in the final tally, was one of the most expensive and overbudget sets built for the film. Beyond the Robbins propensity for change-it or do-it-again, there were also delays caused by the purely human factor of perspiration, which necessitated constant drying out and the occasional change of wardrobe. Additionally, that rooftop set had a rooftop floor: tar paper, which under the many lights could occasionally cause the cast's shoes to remain earthbound. Also in the earthbound category: Rita Moreno, in the final shot of the women perched up on

the men's shoulders. For take after take she would hit her mark atop Chakiris, then feel herself slowly sliding downward. "You know you think of your feet, your toes, trying to hold your balance sometimes? My behind was trying to do that, and it didn't have fingers to latch on to George's shoulders!"

The next major sequence to go before the cameras was possibly the most demanding number of all. "Cool" was shot on what was, bar none, the single most uncomfortable set, wide (85 by 150 feet) of dimension and low (8 feet) of ceiling. Leven's garage was difficult to light and, for the dancers, a performance space resembling a hellish sauna. Moved to a later and more dramatically relevant place in the story, it had an urgency greater than what had been the case onstage. Riff, who

ABOVE & OPPOSITE: "Cool."

had sung it in the play, was now dead so, post-Rumble, the appropriately named Ice incited the Jet men and women to a revenge served cold. It was, literally, dance as drama, and Robbins's direction here was at its zenith, with hot-to-cold movements revealing the Jets' psychology more expressively than could any of the characters' limited language skills.

"Cool" was one of the numbers for which, during rehearsals, Robbins had devised and taught the cast numerous versions and variations. He then had the dancers perform them so he could pick, evaluate, and choose. According to Gina Trikonis, "We were supposed to be able to pull out of our heads the one he wanted to see in an instant—be it version one or twelve, or any in between. For the life of me, I don't know how we kept

them all separate in our heads and bodies and then gave him what he wanted on demand."

Over and over again they would do it, first on the concrete floor of the rehearsal hall and then on Stage 4 in that set, where the banks of lights caused the temperature to soar to near-unbearable levels. Between takes the cast rushed out into the fresh and sometimes chilly California air, then back to the garage, and this in-and-out eventually gave Eliot Feld pneumonia. As if the set and the climate were not difficult enough, Robbins had devised his most physically challenging moves for "Cool," and naturally the difficulty of the choreography found a corollary in the number of takes. The dancers spent hours, days even, down on their knees, and found to their great pain that the knee pads they wore offered precious little protection. Finally, after the directors ordered "Print" for the last time, they gathered up those pads for a ceremonial bonfire. Most accounts add the unsurprising detail that the blaze occurred in front of Robbins's office.

The aching knees, sore muscles, and pneumonia were not isolated cases by any means. Susan Oakes's knee was punctured by a nail when she jumped down onto the floor, and there were countless torn ligaments, sprains, shin splints, scrapes, and burns, as well as dehydration and mononucleosis. The casualty list grew so long that Saul Chaplin suspected some kind of jinx. Robert Relyea—a veteran of such intense projects as *The Alamo, The Magnificent Seven,* and *The Great Escape* (1963)—later offered the assessment that "I don't ever believe I've been on a picture, and I've been on some pretty big action pictures, where there were so many injuries." Not that the dancers would ever think of quitting. For them, hurting was part of the job, and the pain of "Cool" had been more than exceeded by sheer exhilaration and the knowledge that they were creating something spectacular. Their injuries did, however, necessitate some frequent schedule-juggling and additional late-night rehearsals involving cast members who were, on any given day, still standing. There were also times when it was necessary to use body doubles, as when Gina Trikonis was hospitalized with mononucleosis during the filming of "Gee, Officer

Krupke" and, suddenly, Graziella's face is no longer visible.

None of this had any kind of dampening effect on the dancers' high spirits or propensity for mischief. In their time off the lot, they partied and drove recklessly, and things were not always much more disciplined at the studio. In spite of Relyea's incessant admonishments about conserving their energies for their time on camera, they were constantly carousing, playing, and pranking. At one point, between takes, several of the men found some three-wheeled light stands not in use. With cries of "I'm Spartacus!" they began holding chariot races down the streets of the Goldwyn lot. The fun continued at an ever-louder rate until Billy Wilder, working in one of the studio offices, complained of the noise and had the competition shut down.

The mischief-making was hardly confined to the male cast members. Susan Oakes's propensity for practical jokes earned her the title "The Bad Seed," while Yvonne Othon developed an "anything for a laugh" strategy that sometimes involved hanging from the rafters to startle fellow cast members. Much of the misbehavior continued to be directed to head disciplinarian Robert Relyea, and at one point Natalie Wood teamed with Jets Tony Mordente and Tucker Smith to torment him. Wood, wearing Maria's immaculate white dress, lay down on the floor of her dressing room and directed Mordente and Smith to pour ketchup on her. Holding a knife near the spill, she phoned Relyea, who was having a particularly stressful day, screaming for help. The assistant director raced over to her dressing room and, to his horror, saw what appeared to be a stabbing victim. Then all three pranksters yelled "Surprise!" Such things would have given Relyea a bad ulcer had he not already acquired one during the making of *The Alamo*.

STAR WARS

For Natalie Wood, the production's star and latecomer, pranks were a brief respite from a host of responsibilities and challenges. Keenly aware of her "name" status, she could seem to some as aloof, excessively regal, self-contained, even oblivious. Mostly it was a façade, behind which she was insecure and in desperate need of reassurance. Her lunch breaks were often spent on phone calls to her analyst, and there were days when she felt burdened to the point of calling in sick and staying home. Despite some early dance training and her catch-up rehearsal, she remained aware that her dancing lacked the skill of most of the cast. She did, however, earn the dancers' gratitude through a positive demonstration of star power. One day she arrived for a dance rehearsal in a space that was hot to the point of being unbearable. After asking the dancers how they could put up with these conditions, she marched to a

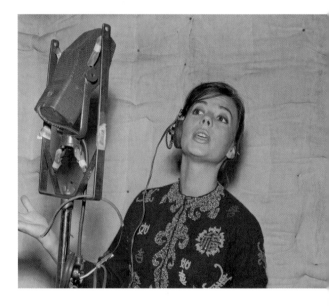

TOP: Touching up Natalie Wood's makeup

MIDDLE: Natalie Wood recording Maria's songs

BOTTOM: During a dance rehearsal, Natalie Wood looks at Yvonne Othon and her cigarette.

ABOVE: In the bridal shop between takes of "I Feel Pretty," with Suzie Kaye, Yvonne Othon, Natalie Wood, and Joanne Miya

telephone. "This is Natalie," she announced, and didn't need to give a last name. "I want air conditioners in the rehearsal hall, a table with coffee, some snacks, and cold water." In a short time, it was all done.

There were two areas in particular that posed challenges for Wood. One was Maria's Puerto Rican accent. In spite of coaching and suggestions from Rita Moreno and Yvonne Othon, she continued to struggle with the accent through the entire shoot. Nor was everyone happy with the result. "Awful" was the blunt word Moreno used to describe it to a Wood biographer. "It could have been really so much better." The other issue was the singing. She had long wanted to sing on film and once, following some voice lessons, had even toyed with the idea of a song-and-dance nightclub act. There had also been

that televised duet with Frank Sinatra, in which her eagerness to please is quite touching. As she continued to work with voice coach Bobby Tucker, she recorded Maria's songs and, during filming, performed to her own playbacks. It soon became apparent that her enthusiasm over her vocals was not always shared by others. At one point, after she excitedly played one of her vocal tracks for costar Russ Tamblyn, the actor's diplomatic response was an exterior smile and an interior wince.

Through the entire filming, Wood remained under the impression that her vocals were to be used in the final film. As Robert Wise commented later, for public consumption, "It looked as if she might be able to do her own singing." The only exception, she believed, would be some high notes supplied by Marni Nixon, an accomplished and busy singer who had already done a few high-profile jobs of ghost singing. This may have been a case of deliberate miscommunication, for Wood's determination to do her own vocals flew in the face of Saul Chaplin's advocacy of, and propensity for, voice doubling. Chaplin, as previously noted, was the man in charge of pairing Al Jolson's off-screen voice with Larry Parks's on-screen lip movements. That, more than anything else, had been responsible for the smash hit of *The Jolson Story*, and for much of Chaplin's subsequent success. To him, faces and voices were separate entities that could be mixed and matched at will for the potential betterment of the production. Natalie Wood was a box-office name, but so was Deborah Kerr, whose vocals had been expertly dubbed by Marni Nixon in *The King and I*. The difference was that Kerr had been aware from the start that she would not be doing her own singing. Nixon was present when Wood recorded her songs for *West Side Story*, and in her memoirs recounted a dispiriting scene:

The entire music department, from Johnny Green to Saul Chaplin to Bobby Tucker, all kept telling Natalie how wonderful her takes were, when it was very evident they were mostly unusable. They also explained my presence [in the recording studio] by saying that they would be able to mix my high notes into her takes. . . . I am sure, however, that they thought if they were critical of her vocals in any way that she would walk off the picture before everything was filmed. She had them hostage and they were placating her until they didn't need her anymore.

According to Nixon, the same people who were praising Wood for her singing would then turn their backs and, to Nixon, give a sly wink.

It was not until much later that Wood learned, to her immense displeasure, that Nixon would be doing all of Maria's singing. Some of Wood's recorded tracks for *West Side Story* survive, and they indeed sound the least effective in the higher reaches of the music, where she had been alerted that Nixon might be doing some fill-in. Unfortunately, they do not always sound convincing in their lower ranges, either. As recorded, her voice does not have the heft sufficient to traverse Maria's more challenging vocal lines, the tone sometimes thins out, and some notes stray from the pitch. A light number such as "I Feel Pretty" works considerably better, and had these recordings been made in a more technologically sophisticated time, it all could have ended differently. With the right kind of enhancement, Wood might have sounded like a plausible Maria, not simply a sincere and underpowered performer. In that scenario, the battle could have been won by the star, not the associate producer.

Through the various pressures she was facing, as well as a lack of personal chemistry, Wood found little rapport with either Richard Beymer or Robert Wise. In no way did the romance between Maria and Tony find an equivalent off camera, and some in the company were heard to say that Wood's indifference toward Beymer sprang from her annoyance that Robert Wagner had not been

cast as Tony. Whatever the reasons behind it, Wood's coolness to Beymer did not add to a sense of passion on the screen; nor did Beymer feel able to break through the wall. Maria and Tony work, as a couple, because of the music, writing, and direction, not because of the spontaneous combustion that ought to be felt between two great lovers. Instead of that, there is a kind of generalized sweetness that some may find a little disappointing. Perhaps this insufficient chemistry may also be due to Robert Wise's approach to actors. Wood, like a few other cast members, found Wise to be unnervingly reticent, a competent commander-in-chief but nothing like an inspiring director. Instead, for the guidance and reassurance she wanted and needed, she turned to Jerome Robbins.

The connection that Natalie Wood did not feel with either Beymer or Wise she found in abundance with Robbins. She was elated that someone of his talent and achievement valued her ability, and he was enchanted with her. Essentially, he treated her as he did one of his special ballerinas, and under his guidance, she developed a physical characterization that proved to be more convincing than her vocal inflections. Their work together was close and at times intense, artistically fulfilling and personally complicated. Such situations were a way of life for Robbins, who fell into the category,

TOP: Natalie Wood (cigarette in hand) and Richard Beymer between takes

BOTTOM: Natalie Wood as Maria

not uncommon in the 1940s, '50s, and '60s, of a neurotic man seeking the right woman to "rescue" him from being gay. Along with his string of male lovers, he had over the years become fascinated with and sometimes engaged to several women, usually dancers. This was not bisexuality as it is now understood; rather, it served as an attempt to eradicate and conquer something inexorable that was also held to be immoral and, at the time, illegal. Wood's personal assistant, Mart Crowley, could see very clearly what was going on between the actress and her director/mentor: "In a way, he *fell* for her . . . and who wouldn't? She was just so captivating, it was almost impossible not to. But Natalie was very hip, and she knew all about Jerry . . . She just knew that she had to handle that relationship very, very carefully because she didn't want to humiliate him or alienate him—and she was crazy about him."

Wood managed to negotiate that dynamic with such grace that the pair remained good friends until her death.

"DO IT AGAIN"

From September into October, through "America" and "Cool," and on to the bridal shop for "I Feel Pretty," the pace of shooting continued at the same rate. Wise offered quiet suggestions and stood by stoically, and Robbins did what he did. Much later, with typical understatement, Wise described the Robbins style as "very demanding, very

demanding, very demanding, do it again, do it again, doing it again. . . . It was wondrous, exasperating, sometimes maddening." Mart Crowley, observing the codirectors at work, noticed something else:

Jerry just didn't pay any attention to Bob Wise whatsoever. It was beyond humiliation, it was that he did not exist on the soundstage. Jerry just took the [view] finder and went and set up the shots and didn't refer to him. I suppose they chatted and talked about what pieces of film they needed. But you didn't get the sense that anybody was running the show except Jerry Robbins on the stage. And Bob Wise was just sitting on the sidelines.

Directorial rapport or no, the quality of the work was self-evident. So was the cost. On a typical large-scale production of the time (and later), the general rule of thumb for shooting was an average of two to four script pages per day, totaling roughly three minutes. This had been the approximate basis for that hopeful ten-week calculation that Relyea had done back in June. By October 10, after "Cool" had been completed, the average on *West Side Story* was less than one page and well under one minute per day. Granted, a dance-heavy musical with a great deal of location work naturally required more time and a slower pace, which was small comfort to those keeping their eyes on the costs. In a way, it all seemed to sum up one downside of independent cinema: something outstanding was being made, beyond the capabilities of the big-studio system, at a cost that was rapidly becoming untenable. A comparison with the ultimate "dream factory" musical is

DATE	SET AND SCENES	LOCATION	CAST
Thursday Dec. 22 thru Tuesday Dec. 27 (Cont'd)	INT. DOC'S CANDY STORE Sc. 106 - NIGHT 5 3/8 Pages - 1/2 Day Anita harassed by Jets tells them Maria is dead. MUSIC: "TAUNTING"	Stage 5	Anita Ice Anybodys All Jets Doc

---

Monday Dec. 26	HOLIDAY		

DATE	SET AND SCENES	LOCATION	CAST
Wednesday Dec. 28 thru Wednesday Jan. 4	INT. DOC'S CANDY STORE Sc. 71 - NIGHT 1/4 Page - 1/4 Day Tony finishes work singing "Tonight." MUSIC: "TONIGHT"	Stage 5	Tony
	EXT. REAR OF DOC'S CANDY STORE Sc. 43 - DAY 4 3/4 Pages - 2 Days Riff talks Tony into coming to dance that night. MUSIC: SOMETHING'S COMING	Ext. Studio	Riff Tony Extras
	EXT. REAR OF DOC'S CANDY STORE Sc. 74 - NIGHT 3/4 Pages - 1/4 Day Jets on the move sing "Tonight." MUSIC: "TONIGHT	Ext. Studio	Riff All Jets Extras

---

(CONTINUED)

instructive. Nine years earlier, *Singin' in the Rain*—with its musical numbers, large-scale ballet, and detailed evocation of an earlier era—had been shot at MGM in a total of fifty-four days. At the end of the day on October 10, *West Side Story* had been in front of the cameras for forty-two days, for a total of thirty-six minutes and twenty-three seconds of film: less than one-quarter of the total running time.

Time was not the only factor escalating the budget. By early October, the cost of the sets was around $100,000 over the original estimate, and several were yet to be completed. The costumes, too, were proving to be more expensive than once envisioned. In addition to the multiple copies required for dance scenes, there was that old-Hollywood need to have outfits tailor-made to look like they had been purchased off the rack. Weeks before the company began to shoot the dance at the gym, the cost for the costumes for that one sequence was being calculated at a steep $68,205.00. (For the record: Wood's and Moreno's dresses were the most expensive among the women's, at about $4,000 each. The priciest men's wear, at $933, was the outfit worn by Russ Tamblyn, with its distinctively natty black collar.)

On October 5, Harold Mirisch sent another of his memos to Wise, Robbins, and production manager Al Wood. "Cool," he noted, had been due to be finished the

following day, but the slow progress thus far indicated that this likely would not happen. He then added, tersely: "Want you to know that whether it ['Cool'] is finished or not, as far as I am concerned we will do no further work on it, and I will expect that the 'Bridal Shop Number' be started on Friday [October 7]."

By the following week, as work continued at the same rate, Mirisch attempted to set markers for the scenes in the bridal shop. "Under no circumstances," he wrote, "can I have the shooting of this number continue past Friday [October 14]." His warnings were heeded on at least one anomalous day, October 20, when a whopping three minutes and fifty-five seconds of footage was captured. At over four times the average figure, this would be the highest daily quota in the entire production. So it continued, with cost overages being noted in all areas—sets, costumes, raw film, and on and on.

Robbins's approach to the filming continued unchanged: meticulous, detailed, insightful, using vast quantities of rehearsal time and film stock, continuing to insist on shooting a scene from multiple angles in order to have more options. Assistant choreographer Margaret Banks recalled that even if a take were unusable due to some error or glitch, Robbins would order, "Print it anyway. I want to look at it." Harold Mirisch had issued a warning about this early on: "I want to caution you [Robbins and Wise] about alternate versions. I realize that more of these were undoubtedly necessary for the

OPPOSITE: A page from the post-Robbins shooting schedule. The actual shooting dates of these scenes were pushed back into January.

Prologue than they will be elsewhere in the story but they are film and time consuming and our budget and schedule just don't allow for them as a regular pattern of shooting. Please exercise strict control over this kind of multiple coverage."

Mirisch was doing what executives are wont to do, while Robbins was being the archetypal brilliant artist, heedful of the final result, oblivious to time and expense. Between them was Robert Wise, who had overseen nearly every aspect of the planning and had, since then, taken what appeared to many as a subsidiary role in actually directing the film. On the set, as Mart Crowley noted, he could be reserved nearly beyond comprehension, seemingly unwilling, or at least hesitant, to give direction. His directorial style had always been one of quiet authority; here, to some on the set, it seemed less authoritative than disengaged. About the only instruction he would give to the Jets and the Sharks was, "Don't lose your New York accent." Tony Mordente, for one, felt that Robert Relyea was doing more of the directing than Wise. This may have been something of an illusion. As both codirector and credited producer, it was necessary for his feet to be planted in the camps of both art and commerce, and perhaps he was not unwilling to continue quietly in "wait and see" mode. Meanwhile, from the initial rosy projection of around $4.5 million, the budget had soared well past $5 million; ultimately, it would reach the total, per Walter Mirisch, of $6.75 million. This overrun was far less drastic than several out-of-control productions of the same time, such as *One-Eyed Jacks* (1961), *Mutiny on the Bounty* (1962), and, inevitably, *Cleopatra* (1963). Still, *West Side Story* would be the most costly film released in 1961, and there was about to be a major change.

THE RUMBLE

The change, of course, was Robbins's dismissal from the film in the latter part of October 1960. Even to many people not versed in behind-the-scenes movie lore, it's well known that Jerome Robbins was fired from *West Side Story* midway through production. This is not necessarily an unheard-of kind of event; many major films—*The Wizard of Oz, Gone With the Wind* (1939), *Spartacus*— had directors who were discharged shortly after production began. There are also, from *Mister Roberts* (1955) to *Bohemian Rhapsody* (2018), numerous instances of major projects changing directors midway through filming, or later. The unique aspect here lay in Robbins's connection with *West Side Story*, which went beyond mere experience to near-absolute dominion. Protectively and defensively, Robbins regarded *West Side Story* as his creation, his vision, his responsibility. He had overseen every aspect of the Broadway production and, for film, he could not do any less. Never mind that the motion picture was a medium with which he had had only slight previous contact. For him, a film

set served the same function as a stage that had been prepared for a dress rehearsal—it was ready in some particulars and usually in desperate need of a great deal of further work. Unlike live performance, film was permanent, allowing for no deviation from the perfect. "It's there forever," he had told his Jets when commanding them to do another take, and for him that was a mandate for the fiercest application of trial and error imaginable. Never mind the budget, the cost of Panavision 70 film stock, the quiet presence of Robert Wise alongside him, or the number of Mirisches counting the number of takes. Never mind, even, human frailty, endurance, or possible injury. The final result, which would bear his name, was what counted.

Much later, Robert Relyea described Robbins's dismissal as a "coup" and an "assassination" that was "planned down to the finest detail." That is a harsh way to put it, yet it does not seem to have been a hasty or capricious act. Walter Mirisch recounted in his memoirs that the trouble was obvious early on and that "We concentrated on getting as many of the musical numbers shot as early in the schedule as we could." Of course it had been necessary to shoot the Prologue first because of both weather and impending building demolition, and "America," "Cool," "I Feel Pretty," and "One Hand,

TOP: Jerome Robbins and Robert Wise—one directing, the other observing

MIDDLE: Robert Wise directs Richard Beymer and Natalie Wood in the bridal shop.

BOTTOM: Robert Wise directs Russ Tamblyn in the gym.

One Heart" were all completed. Except for the gym sequence and the "Somewhere" dream ballet, the remaining numbers were not heavy on dance. Essentially, Wise could direct them on his own, with Robbins's assistants helping with the staging.

According to Walter Mirisch, the decision began with him and his brothers, followed by a discussion with Wise. Wise was willing to continue with the codirector setup, but concurred that Robbins's assistants could take over for him if he left. With that, Mirisch asked Robbins's agent to be the bearer of the bad news. The agent refused, and it was on a weekend that Harold and Walter Mirisch drove to Robbins's rented house in Beverly Hills to inform him that he was discharged. It was, as Mirisch had anticipated, "a terrible scene." Along with the expected rage and hurt, Robbins expressed the desire to sever ties completely. According to Mirisch, "He told us that if he was let go, he wanted to take his name off the picture. I didn't want him to do that and replied, 'Of course, that's your prerogative. But I suggest that you wait until the picture is finished, and then decide whether or not it is so far afield from what you would have wanted.'"

Agreeing to that final suggestion, Robbins began preparing to return East. It was now left to Relyea and others to pass along the word of his dismissal. As Robbins's chief assistant, Howard Jeffrey would now be appointed main choreographer, but when Relyea told him of his new assignment, Jeffrey reacted with tears, a well-aimed obscenity, a slammed door, and a permanent exit from the studio.

Russ Tamblyn heard the news early on and expected that other cast members, particularly the dancers, would greet the change with relief. Instead, he was surprised to find most of them reacting with outrage, disbelief, and gut-punched devastation. Several of them have recalled that they learned of the dismissal on the gym set, where they had been rehearsing. It had only been a few days earlier that they had experienced one of Robbins's worst scenes. "None of you can dance!" he had yelled at them. "Each and every one of you can be replaced!" Now he was gone, and, for them, there could be no *West Side Story* without Jerome Robbins. There were thoughts, in some of the dancers' minds, of walking out. Finally, it occurred to them that it was their responsibility to realize the Robbins vision, and so they all stayed. Natalie Wood's reaction was one of unbridled fury, and she threatened to leave as well, at least until her agent (and, reportedly, Robbins) convinced her otherwise. Much of the guidance she had sought from Robbins would now be given to her by Tony Mordente, newly (if reluctantly) promoted to the position of dance assistant alongside Tommy Abbott (Gee-Tar) and Margaret Banks. They were now charged with translating the remainder of Robbins's rehearsals into finished, filmed performances.

Robert Wise's role in the termination is one of its most striking ambiguities. It was Mart Crowley's perception that Wise, when codirecting alongside Robbins, "was just sitting there waiting, waiting, waiting until his moment . . . to lower the boom." Yet Saul Chaplin later said that Wise fought to keep Robbins as codirector. Wise was completely aware that Robbins possessed ample gifts that he himself did not—an abundant dance vocabulary, the ability to express a character's psychology through stylized movement, the gift for creating coherent musical numbers out of a mosaic of small film pieces. Wise relied heavily on these assets and, since domination and control were Robbins's natural state, it often appeared that he was letting Robbins take over. This kind of recessiveness makes for an arresting contrast with Wise's hands-on approach during its preparation and casting, as well as his detailed work, after shooting, with special-effects supervisor Linwood Dunn and other technicians.

As it happened, Wise had already played a role in another major cinematic termination: Orson Welles's post-shoot removal from *The Magnificent Ambersons* (1942), in 1942, which was done after Welles had left the country and his studio (RKO) decided that the film was far too long. It was left to Wise, as editor, to assemble a drastically shorter and recut version, which included some new footage he directed. Welles regarded this as betrayal and vandalism, and Wise could later be somewhat defensive about *Ambersons*. His comments to a Welles biographer were both revealing and, in light of the Robbins affair, quite apt: "[*Ambersons*] probably was a better picture in its original-length version: as an accomplishment. . . .

But we were faced with the reality of not art but business, and what to do with something that wouldn't play. . . . I can tell you, everybody strived as hard as they could to retain every bit of the feeling, the quality of what Orson was trying to do."

The parallels between Orson Welles and Jerome Robbins are obvious: both were driven men from the East, regarded as species of "genius," being compelled to play Hollywood games of budget and schedules. Both paid the price for their achievements. And with both of them, it was Robert Wise, a master of reassuring, even-keeled competence, who was assigned to sweep up and smooth over.

One major casualty of Robbins's departure was the "Somewhere" dream ballet. From early on, it had been included in all the script drafts, yet never with any kind of specificity in the script or the production correspondence. A memo from Wise to Relyea in June of 1960 indicates how it was being approached: "The ballet should be put at the end of the schedule to give Mr. Robbins as much time as possible to plan it." Robbins's rehearsals prior to filming had been devoted to the other numbers, and it appears that even then the number was being retained on a kind of contingency basis, to be filmed if the schedule and budget permitted. Perhaps it was thought that Wise could continue with the dramatic scenes while Robbins went off to conceive and stage the ballet. Something similar had happened a decade earlier with Gene Kelly's staging of the ballet sequence in

ABOVE: Russ Tamblyn filmed "Jet Song" to his own recording—a situation which changed for the completed film.

BELOW: "Gee, Officer Krupke": David Bean, Bert Michaels, Russ Tamblyn, and Anthony Teague

OPPOSITE: Fun off camera, with Russ Tamblyn, Sue Oakes, and George Chakiris

PREVIOUS PAGE: Tony (Beymer) and Bernardo (Chakiris) start to rumble.

ABOVE: Richard Beymer as Tony ("Something's Coming")

BELOW: Tommy Abbott, Richard Beymer, and Natalie Wood taking a break during rehearsal of the final scene. Note the Zuberano storyboard panel between Beymer and Wood.

OPPOSITE: Assistant director (and disciplinarian-in-chief) Robert Relyea, with crew and Jets

PREVIOUS PAGE: Bernardo (Chakiris) with his switchblade (left), Riff (Tamblyn) with his switchblade (right)

ABOVE: "Cool"

BELOW: "America": George Chakiris and the Sharks, Joanne Miya, Yvonne Othon, Rita Moreno, Maria Juminez, Suzie Kaye

OPPOSITE: "One Hand, One Heart": Tony and Maria

PREVIOUS PAGE: The end of the Rumble: George Chakiris, Richard Beymer, Russ Tamblyn, Jets and Sharks

ABOVE: Rita Moreno in the bridal shop

OPPOSITE: Marni Nixon with her score of "I Feel Pretty"

An American in Paris, but that was at MGM, at a time when the musical assembly line could allow for such complexities. With *West Side Story*, a stand-alone enterprise, it was clear early on that there was never going to be time for the ballet. By the beginning of November, any mention of it had been scratched off the shooting script and the schedule.

THE NATURE OF THE BEAST

Work moved forward following the big shake-up at a slightly faster clip, at least on the more productive days. Nevertheless, there was, and would always be, the inherent character of the production: it was a large, complex, and draining project being shot independently under the supervision of people who were not, except for Saul Chaplin, always attuned to the special needs of musical filmmaking. The slow pace of the shooting was, in Wise's words, "just the nature of the beast." Delays were the rule more than the exception, and accidents and injuries continued to occur without cease. Less visible injuries were there as well in the quiet division that was present on the set: Wood and many of the dancers remained loyal to Robbins, while Relyea and most of the crew favored Wise. Some, like Carole D'Andrea, stayed in the middle. She and Robbins had enormous mutual respect, in part because he knew she wasn't afraid of him, yet she also bonded with Wise. No, she says, Wise, "didn't do much direction personally," but

he did know film. "I loved that dear gifted man."

For Richard Beymer, this biggest professional opportunity to date was something of a dispiriting experience. Tony Mordente, among others, observed both the situation vis-à-vis Natalie Wood and the actor's ongoing uncertain grasp on his role. "I felt sorry for Richard," Mordente said, "because he was really miscast and he really felt ill-at-ease doing the whole movie." Robert Wise had viewed Beymer as the best of all the prospective Tonys, as did Saul Chaplin. ("Far and away," Chaplin insisted, "the best actor we tested for the role.") Between auditions and actual filming, however, there may have been a change, prompted by insufficient guidance, an uninterested costar, and possibly, as Mordente observed, some personal dissatisfaction. Three decades later, after finding that he preferred filmmaking to acting, Beymer gave his take on the role and the performance: "It's a thankless role [and] could have been played more street-wise, with someone other than me, who was born in Iowa and didn't have a clue as to what New York was all about. What would De Niro have done with a part like that?"

Early in November, there was another round of location work, far more concise than the first, if similarly snail-paced. Wise and the crew, plus Tamblyn, Chakiris, and the Jets and Sharks, trooped to downtown Los Angeles for four nights of filming under highway overpasses. The scenes were entirely contained in the latter sections of the "Tonight Quintet," ultimately occupying less than thirty seconds of screen time. The company then moved to the gym, where rehearsals had already been going on for some time. As the biggest musical sequence that Robbins did not codirect with Wise, it would not, upon close examination, have the degree of dance-as-cinema virtuosity and dynamic editing that "Cool" had, or the Prologue. What it did have was some of the most astute choreography, including Russ Tamblyn giving stunning testament to the corollary between gymnastic ability and dance skill. Tamblyn's tumble/twist/backflip, one of the pieces added by Tony Mordente, gave the film one of its single most exhilarating moments.

While the gym number proceeded essentially as planned, the set was not free from tension. Both Natalie Wood and the majority of the dancers felt Robbins's absence acutely, and Wood required numerous takes to get her steps right. Her concentration on her work was seen by some cast members as a kind of detached indifference, and her ongoing lack of rapport with Beymer was not so much observed as felt. One of Wood's coping mechanisms, Tamblyn recalled, involved keeping on her dressing room wall a document alternately referred to as an "'S' list" or a "hit list." (It's safe to assume that, at some point, those two designated titles were combined.) Beymer's name was one of those mentioned, for reasons unspecified.

BELOW: Russ Tamblyn in midair, with Sue Oakes, Gina Trikonis, Carole D'Andrea, and the Jets and the Sharks

PAGES 125–126: The Jets take off at the gym, with Russ Tamblyn and Gina Trikonis in the foreground and John Astin at the rear.

"You didn't have to do much [to get on it]," Tamblyn said, "You could get on that list for *not* doing something."

After work finished in the gym, the shooting proceeded onward at the same slow-but-steady rate. The days of multiple delays and low footage counts continued, and even with the scrapping of the "Somewhere" ballet, the schedule stretched out ever farther. The love scene on the balcony, the scenes in Maria's apartment, "Gee, Officer Krupke," "The Rumble," the remaining parts of "Jet Song," shot outdoors at the Goldwyn studio—all of them went relatively smoothly, yet far over the time originally allotted. Early in November, after Robbins left, Relyea had carefully laid out the schedule and calculated that shooting would conclude on January 4. It was,

yet again, a case of extreme optimism. By the time 1961 arrived, much remained to be filmed.

For Rita Moreno, the most harrowing part of the filming came in January with the "Taunting" scene, in which Anita goes to Doc's to deliver a message from Maria to Tony and narrowly escapes gang rape by the Jets. Between the complicated staging, the escalating intensity, and the sheer unpleasantness, it was the emotional equivalent of the physical hurts inflicted in shooting the "Cool" number. Moreno quickly found that her identification with the scene went far beyond lines being read from a script page. "I *was* Anita, in a way [and] she was me . . . the girl that the kids called Spic and Garlic Mouth and Gold Tooth." Finally,

BELOW: Difficult to film, difficult to watch: the Jets maul Anita. Bert Michaels, Robert Banas, Anthony Teague, Harvey Hohnecker, Eliot Feld (hidden), Rita Moreno, David Bean, Tony Mordente (hidden), and Tommy Abbott.

between takes, Moreno reached a breaking point and began to weep uncontrollably. The Jets, already unsettled by the lines and actions they were being given to do, rushed over to comfort her and give her the assurance that the audience would indeed hate them for what they were doing to her on-screen. Finally, Wise called for a break to allow Moreno time to pull herself together. The scene was delayed additionally when Moreno, about to shoot Anita's final lines, asked Wise to be excused for a minute. She darted off, intending to run around the huge soundstage to get herself in a breathless, agitated mood. When she failed to return, it was Relyea who found her lying on the floor, tangled in cables.

Finally, on February 14, day 124 of filming, it was done. A wrap party followed, with the expected high spirits on the part of the Jets and the Sharks, including further, final attempts at shaving. There was, all told, a good deal to celebrate: not including any of the rehearsals, tests, preparation, or post-production, the shoot had taken more than six months. Not that it was anywhere near done. Much, much work remained, including some process shots of Richard Beymer for "Maria" that were filmed later in the spring. Much of the responsibility lay with Wise and Chaplin, and as they each continued their dauntingly long lists of tasks, they began to share a catchphrase: "Chipping away at it."

A large amount of Chaplin's remaining work came with the music tracks, and some of that work was not pleasant. According to

multiple reports, it was at the end of filming that Natalie Wood learned that her vocals were to be completely scrapped in favor of new ones to be done by Marni Nixon. Nixon's job was going to be far more difficult than simply singing, since it would involve her needing to match her phrasing with Wood's filmed performances—a kind of dubbing in reverse. Wood's reaction was comparable to that of her learning of the Robbins dismissal, perhaps with an even greater feeling of betrayal. Assured repeatedly that her recordings had been more than acceptable, she was now confronted with what felt like an especially personal kind of rejection. It was a sour conclusion to a difficult professional experience and, as reported by Mart Crowley, she never forgave Robert Wise. Chaplin, for his part, said later that he had known from the beginning that Wood's singing could not be used.

Wood's was hardly the only voice Chaplin replaced. Jimmy Bryant had already recorded Tony's music, and although Richard Beymer once mentioned to Marni Nixon that he would have liked an opportunity to do the vocals himself, he had performed to Bryant's tracks. Anita's songs were ultimately the work of three singers: Rita Moreno, who sang "America" and most of the "Tonight Quintet"; Betty Wand, who filled in for Moreno (unsatisfactorily, in Moreno's opinion) on "A Boy Like That"; and Marni Nixon, who filled in the high notes near the end of the "Tonight Quintet" when both Moreno and Wand were unavailable. Chaplin's drive

for vocal perfection could be relentless and even ruthless. Having decided that he did not care for Russ Tamblyn's performance of "Jet Song," Chaplin began to look elsewhere for a vocalist. Oddly enough, he turned to Tucker Smith, who had already done his own singing in the role of Ice. After learning that Smith could do an expert imitation of Tamblyn, Chaplin had him do a recording, and Smith's "Jet Song" is the one used in the film. Tamblyn's performance also survives and, in truth, the two renditions sound quite similar. The main difference between them is that Smith's singing has a little more polish while Tamblyn's is scrappier and more characterful. Chaplin did allow Tamblyn to sing "Gee, Officer Krupke" for himself, which makes his decision to replace Tamblyn on "Jet Song" seem, at best, unnecessary.

Clearly, Tamblyn was capable of handling the song.

For Wise, postproduction brought out considerable vigor that had not always been in evidence during filming. As a former editor, he worked closely with Thomas Stanford to assemble the footage, tightening everything but not deleting any significant material; the production had been planned so well that there would be no "cut numbers," nothing to turn up later as supplements on home video. By early April, a rough cut was ready and, as contractually required, shipped to New York for Jerome Robbins to see. The main objection Robbins had, predictably enough, involved the dance number for which he had not been present. In particular, he felt that Tony and Maria's first meeting, at the gym, had lost its urgency:

The main problem of the picture is to fix the Dance Hall sequence. It isn't a question of the dancing or choreography; what's lost is the tense <u>action</u> of plot and story leading to a highly emotional meeting of the lovers.

I cannot express strongly enough how disappointing is the meeting of the two lovers. . . . This was one of the most effective moments on the stage and it is completely missed in the film and becomes prosaic, untouching and insensitive.

He did, however, praise the segue back to reality following Tony and Maria's first meeting, calling it "absolutely brilliant." A lesser liability, for him, was the moving of the balcony scene from its original stage slot, following "Maria," to after "America." All in all, with the exception of the gym scene, Robbins declared himself satisfied with most of the film, adding that "There are many places where I'm just overjoyed with what has been done." He then added something that may have been both a compliment and a dig: "I know you all think that you have a wonderful picture [but] please believe me that all these suggestions can only help improve it." Some of his ideas were heeded: while the balcony scene was kept in its position after "America," there was some re-editing in response to his comments about Tony and Maria meeting at the gym.

Although Robbins proved to be tractable in dealing with the editing, a conflict

TOP: George Chakiris, Rita Moreno, and the Sharks at the gym

BOTTOM: "America": Suzie Kaye, Yvonne Othon, Rita Moreno, and Maria Jimenez, with George Chakiris and the Sharks

PAGES 132–133: The dance at the gym

arose with the question of his billing, both on-screen and in publicity materials. The original contract had stated that Robbins would get three separate credits: for 1) codirecting, 2) choreographing and staging the musical numbers, and 3) his work in conceiving, directing, and choreographing the original show. As postproduction work was going on in April and May of 1961, the normally amenable and gracious Wise asked for a change in the second credit to reflect the fact that Robbins had left before some of the musical numbers were shot:

I feel I am going way past halfway in according co-director credit to a man who was not involved in the filming of 65 to 70% of the picture.

It's true that Jerry rehearsed most of the numbers and was involved in staging five of them for the screen. But he simply was not around for the filming of the balance of the numbers and songs— or the balance of the picture. As co-director he will be getting credit for a great amount of material that he did not rehearse or help in staging.

In the end, the contentious credit read, simply, "Choreography by Jerome Robbins."

The whole subject of screen credit was not merely a matter of contracts and personal pride. It also cut directly to one of the most exacting aspects of the postproduction—the on-screen credits, at the beginning and end, designed by Saul Bass. The opening was entirely unconventional: a newly assembled Bernstein overture played under an abstract group of dots and vertical lines, with a background shifting from one color to another in reflection of the musi-

ABOVE: Jay Norman, George Chakiris, and Gus Trikonis in "America"

OPPOSITE: Natalie Wood, Richard Beymer, and Robert Wise shooting the final scene

cal segues. Finally, the camera pulled back to show "WEST SIDE STORY" written under the design, which then dissolved into the first of Wise's aerial vistas, Manhattan Island looking north from the harbor. The remainder of the credits did not come on-screen until the very end, unlike those of nearly every major American film prior to *West Side Story*. (Among the rare exceptions: the films Wise edited for Orson Welles, *Citizen Kane* and *The Magnificent Ambersons*.) Not that the closing credits were significant for their placement alone; designed to serve as a continuation of the drama, they involved graffiti scrawled on a series of urban walls, fences, doors, and signs, many of them resembling

backgrounds in the film. They were, in fact, real and three-dimensional, a series of nine studio settings with some of the cast and crew names written on the walls. Others, in the tradition of more conventional screen titling, were superimposed. The sequence, backed by a sumptuous medley of the Bernstein melodies, anticipated the mega-credits of later years by running more than five minutes.

The actual execution of the credits, as well as the other optical effects, was entrusted to Linwood G. Dunn and his company, Film Effects of Hollywood. Dunn was one of those behind-the-camera technicians whose work, over many decades, could qualify for the term "wizardry." Starting as a cameraman and quickly moving into special optical work, Dunn shot the RKO studio logo, devised ways to combine the animated King Kong with the real-life Fay Wray, and saw to it that, in *Flying Down to Rio* (1933), a group of women appeared to be dancing on the wings of high-soaring airplanes. He invented special film printers, devised new ways to combine photographic elements, and even came up with a way to shoot actresses' low-cut necklines without the cleavage running afoul of censors. For *West Side Story*, his visual effects—the execution of Bass's designs, Maria's twirl before her first dance, the going-in-and-out of her first meeting with Tony, the modulations of light and color during the two love duets—were, in a pre-digital era, unusually demanding. In his initial proposal to the film company,

Dunn had declared that "Nothing is really impossible in the realm of special effects." Wise, who had worked with Dunn at RKO, evidently took these words to heart, frequently ordering the effects to be corrected, tweaked, or redone completely. The Panavision 70 process had made it necessary for Dunn to build new equipment for shooting and printing, and this all took longer than planned. There were also delays at the Technicolor lab in making the 70mm print to be run at the premiere. From beginning to end, the production had been consistent in that regard.

All told, the production took two years of concentrated work; $6.75 million; hundreds of auditions and tests; injuries without number; two (or one-and-a-half) directors; turmoil and tumult; an astounding amount of horseplay; times of subterfuge and diplomacy; one immense change; large amounts of anger, hurt feelings, and professionalism; and many, many, many rehearsals and takes. The cast and crew finally dispersed, the technical artisans had done everything asked of them, and the publicity people made sure that the world knew about it. On October 18, 1961, at the Rivoli Theatre in Manhattan, *West Side Story* would finally be up there on the screen.

OPPOSITE: Maria's twirling transition from the bridal shop to the gym was one of the most intricate components of postproduction.

PAGES 138-139: The closing credits, as designed by Saul Bass

DIRECTED BY

ROBERT WI

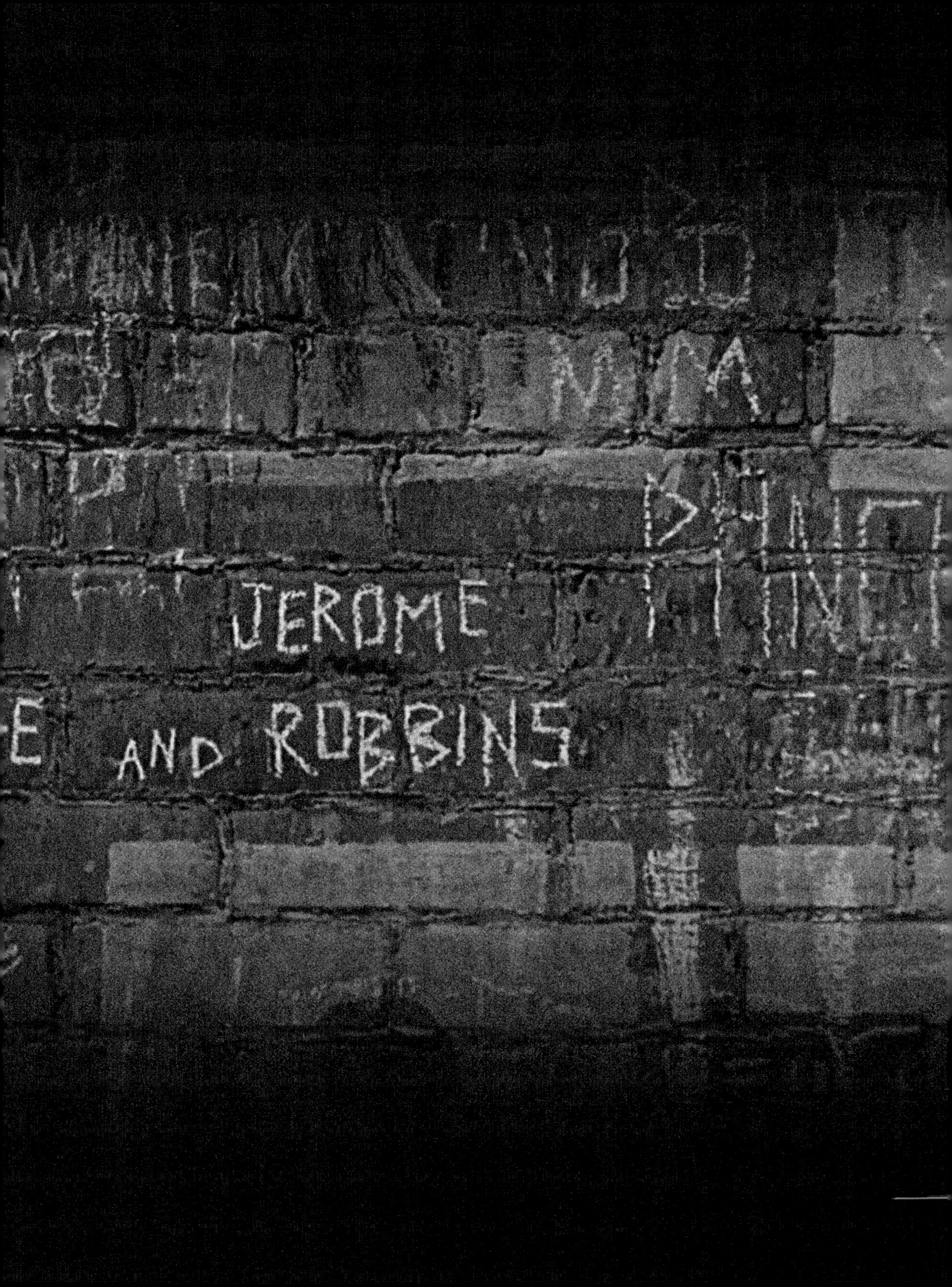
JEROME
AND ROBBINS

INTERMISSION
DIFFERENCES BETWEEN THE STAGE AND FILM VERSIONS OF WEST SIDE STORY

WHILE GENERALLY QUITE faithful to its original source, *West Side Story* did undergo alterations on its way from the stage to the screen. Some met with the approval of the original authors while others did not.

★ Instead of an overture, the original show opened with the curtain rising and the Prologue starting. For the film, an overture preceded the opening montage and Prologue. It consists of the following parts:

  ★ Gang whistle (three times)

  ★ "Tonight Quintet"

  ★ "Tonight"

  ★ "Maria"

  ★ "Dance at the Gym—Mambo"

  ★ "Tonight Quintet" conclusion

★ The aerial montage after the overture was not (and likely could not have been) part of the original show. For the film, it is accompanied by ambient city sounds, more gang whistles, and bongo drums.

★ The Prologue is approximately double the length that it had been on the stage. For a fee of $7,500, Leonard Bernstein was contracted to write new music for this sequence, which would not include more than four minutes of music already composed for the Prologue for the stage.

★ The lyrics of "The Jet Song" and "Gee, Officer Krupke" were both changed (i.e. censored). In the former, "The whole ever mother-lovin' street" became "The whole buggin' ever-lovin'

street." In "Krupke," the original lines went, "My father is a bastard/My ma's an S.O.B./My grandpa's always plastered/My grandma pushes tea." ("Pushing tea" is 1950s slang for "sells marijuana.") In the movie rewrite, "My father beats my mommy/My mommy clobbers me/My grandpa is a Commie," and Grandma was allowed to keep selling herb.

★ On a related note, Tony's friends-for-life pledge to Riff, originally "Sperm to worm," was softened to "Birth to earth."

★ Another substitution in "Krupke" came with swapping "slob" for "schmuck." The latter term, while it has come to mean an obnoxious or useless person, was once a fairly scabrous Yiddish epithet.

★ Both the Jets and the Sharks lost and gained some members. Among the Jets, Diesel was retired in favor of Ice and Joyboy. The Sharks' Anxious, Nibbles, and Moose became, for the film, Loco, Rocco, Del Campo, and Chile.

★ Another character added for the film: Madam Lucia, who owns the bridal shop where Anita and Maria work.

★ In the play, Riff was paired with Velma and Action with Graziella. For the movie, the two Jets swapped romantic partners.

★ In a number of places, the characters were given additional lines of dialogue, intended to flesh out their characters and motivations. Some were written in Ernest Lehman's "final screenplay," while others were added on the set and penciled in by the script supervisor.

★ On the stage, "Tonight" was followed by "America." On film, the two songs switch places, a change which Jerome Robbins did not endorse.

★ "America" was given something approaching a complete overhaul, with a new set of lyrics by Stephen Sondheim. While Anita and the other

OPPOSITE: Rita Moreno in "America," with Jose De Vega, Eddie Verso, and Jaime Rogers

PAGE 141: Gina Trikonis and Russ Tamblyn at the gym, observed by Tucker Smith, David Bean, & Carole D'Andrea

Shark girlfriends sang the number on the stage, the movie expanded it to also include Bernardo and the Sharks. The controversial reference to "tropical diseases" was deleted, and the musical argument between Anita and Rosalia became a back-and-forth between Anita and Bernardo. Many of Anita's original criticisms of Puerto Rico were transformed into praise for America, which Bernardo then countered with put-downs.

* In a move that met with general approval, "Cool" and "Gee, Officer Krupke" swapped places, before and after the Rumble. Riff, not Action, leads "Krupke," with "Cool" now sung by the new Jet, Ice.

* "I Feel Pretty" was shifted to occur before, not after, the Rumble, a move appreciated by some and disputed by others. The time change necessitated new lyrics to indicate "gay" and "today" rather "bright" and "tonight."

* A number of changes in the "Tonight Quintet," including Anita's reference to Bernardo being "hot," which the Production Code people found unacceptable. (Now, instead, he's simply "here.") Maria now sings part of the first chorus of "Tonight" instead of Tony, and many of the lines sung by the Jets and Sharks have been swapped and/or redistributed. Riff's exchange with Tony becomes an exchange with the new character Ice, and the reference to Diesel has been removed (as was that character).

* On the stage, Act I ended after the Rumble. Originally, the plan had been to have the movie break for an intermission as well, followed by a short entr'acte set to "I Feel Pretty." Ultimately, it was decided to continue the dramatic momentum and discard the intermission entirely. For the 2004 DVD release, the intermission break was reinstated, along with the entr'acte. It occurs after Tony strolls into the playground following the war council at Doc's.

* Instead of Consuelo (in the original production), "Somewhere" is now sung by Tony and Maria.

* In the only major deletion of stage material, the "Somewhere" ballet was eliminated.

* The "Taunting" scene between Anita and the Sharks is longer, and even more harrowing, than on the stage. One of the added lines is Rita Moreno's unforgettable "Don't you touch me!"

* In the show, Doc's line to the Sharks, when he finds them about to rape Anita, is "What've you been doing now?" For the film, it became "What are you doing now?" After a preview audience began to laugh at that point, Wise asked Ernest Lehman to write several alternate lines, one of which was "How could you do such a terrible thing!" Then he rejected all of Lehman's options and had Ned Glass (Doc) redub the line as, simply, "What are you doing there?"

* Maria's final speech, to the assembled Jets and Sharks, contains a few changes, including the addition of "Not with bullets and guns—with hate!" What had been "I hate now" in the original script became "I have hate!"

* An "exit" medley was added for the lengthy credit sequence that ends the film. It consists of the following:

  * "Somewhere"

  * "Tonight"

  * "I Feel Pretty"

  * "Maria"

  * "Somewhere" conclusion

OPPOSITE: The Jets and Officer Krupke: Tucker Smith, Eliot Feld, Russ Tamblyn, Bert Michaels, Anthony Teague, William Bramley, and Harvey Hohnecker.

WSS-5

CHAPTER SIX

YES, IT COULD: REACTIONS AND REWARDS

—

"Thank you very much. It's been a wonderfully exciting evening for *West Side Story*."

ROBERT WISE,
accepting the Best Picture Academy Award,
April 9, 1962

ABOVE: The Rivoli Theatre, circa 1957

OPPOSITE: The ad in the *New York Times* three days before the premiere, with the Caroff art

PAGE 146: George Chakiris and Rita Moreno arrive at Grauman's Chinese for the Hollywood premiere.

THE RIVOLI THEATRE, AT 1620 Broadway on the northern end of Times Square, had a Parthenon-like facade and a well-appointed 2,270-seat auditorium. For nearly four decades, it was one of New York's most impressive movie houses. Then, in the mid-1950s, it became something greater. Newly outfitted with the most advanced film tech-nology, the Rivoli was transformed into a tem-ple of cinema culture. Specifically, it became a road-show theater. The road show–film experience, which no longer exists, forms a key part of the saga of *West Side Story*.

Far beyond simply going to a movie, a road show was cinema as Event. It was founded on a psychology completely unlike the movie-watching of a later time, based

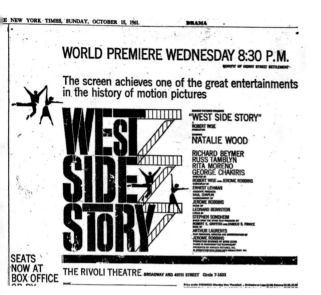

on anticipation and exclusivity instead of immediate gratification. It also put movies on an equal level with live theater. Road-show films played only in a handful of the-aters across the country, with "hard-ticket" reserved seats sold well in advance at ele-vated prices. The screenings were only once or twice per day, and people dressed up—men in coat and tie, women in hats and gloves. There was a glossy souvenir program on sale in the lobby, attendants were on duty in the restrooms, and a staff of uniformed ushers led the spectators to their appointed seats. The projection and sound were han-dled with meticulous care, and there were none of the standard add-ons such as pre-views, cartoons, or shorts. Even the refresh-ments rose above the norm of popcorn and soda. It all functioned, of course, as a way of giving audiences something that made

television look puny. To qualify for a road-show run, a film had to be important, which translated as prestigious and expensive. *Oklahoma!* (1955) and *Around the World in 80 Days* (1956), which both premiered at the Rivoli, were seen to fit that bill. So did *West Side Story.* By this point, due largely to the publicity surrounding the film, the formerly "iffy proposition" was considered a prime movie property. Besides, given its origins and setting, where else could it open but in New York?

Advance marketing was an important part of the road-show proposition. Starting months ahead of the premiere, the United Artists and Mirisch publicists saw to it that *West Side Story* was given a painstaking and extensive campaign. They had the advan-tage of a title that was already familiar, and which bore overtones of quality and "class." Accordingly, most of the advertising bore the lofty (if syntactically questionable) slo-gan "The screen achieves one of the great entertainments in motion picture history." Alongside that, in ads was one of the all-time great movie logos. Erroneously credited to Saul Bass, who had designed the credits, the logo was the work of graphic artist Joseph Caroff. Indeed, it was Caroff's first work in movie advertising, and talk about hitting a homerun the first time at bat. With its blaz-ing-red background, fire escape, abstract dancer silhouettes, and "No Parking"–style black lettering, it was as close to perfect as movie advertising could get. Direct, unclut-tered, and indelible, it was so communi-

cative that Bernstein's music seems to be playing in the distance; small wonder then, that original release posters now go for high prices. Although Caroff later worked only sporadically in film, he also served United Artists well by designing the "007" pistol logo still in use after more than fifty years of James Bond films.

Along with the advertising, United Artists saw to it that the release pattern reflected the exclusivity—entitlement, really—that was key to the whole road-show experience. In the days when a film was not required to pay for itself on four thousand screens in its opening weekend, a prestige title was allowed to gather momentum through the slowest of rollouts. For two weeks after the premiere, the Rivoli was the only theater anywhere running *West Side Story*. Next came Boston, followed later by Philadelphia and Washington, D.C. December 13 saw the opening in Hollywood at Grauman's Chinese Theatre, and then Miami Beach and San Francisco. Eight more cities—including Baltimore, Detroit, and Montreal—would follow in February 1962. In all these cities, the newspaper ads would begin running months ahead of time and included an order blank for tickets. These, for a successful road show, needed to be ordered long in advance. And at $3, the top seats at the Rivoli were nearly five times the average movie-ticket price in 1961.

TOP: Rita Moreno arrives in New York prior to the premiere.

BOTTOM: Warren Beatty escorts Natalie Wood to the Hollywood premiere at Grauman's Chinese.

All this carried a clear message: it took both effort and money to see *West Side Story*, and it would most likely be worth the trouble and expense.

On Wednesday, October 18, 1961, the front page of the *New York Times* forecast warmer temperatures for the next few days, reported America's attempt to dissuade the U.S.S.R. from its plans to detonate a 50-megaton hydrogen bomb, and detailed a plan by the city's mayor, Robert Wagner, to curb crime and juvenile delinquency. On page 48, an ad with the Caroff artwork excitedly announced, "Tonight! Tonight! It all begins tonight!" The premiere was a benefit for the Henry Street Settlement, then and now one of the city's most august charitable organizations. It was, all in all, a reasonably sober occasion, since the flashier, star-filled launch would not be held until December. For Natalie Wood, the night may have marked the moment her star rose to its highest point. *Splendor in the Grass* had just opened and given her the best reviews of her career. Then, eight days later, came the synergy of the year's most eagerly awaited film. There had also been the recent headline-making breakup of her marriage to Robert Wagner (the actor, not the mayor), plus the fact that she was now being escorted by her *Splendor* costar (and former *West Side Story* candidate) Warren Beatty. Eighteen years into her career, this intersection of professional and personal lives had propelled her into top stardom. News photos of the Rivoli opening reveal an arresting intersection of popular culture and current events: Natalie Wood, glamorous in her strapless gown, posing with United Nations Secretary-General U Thant and the U.N.'s American ambassador, Adlai Stevenson.

For Rita Moreno, too, who attended the premiere with George Chakiris, there was a newly minted burst of publicity. She also had been working since childhood, and the quality of her performance as Anita guaranteed that she would be getting positive attention far beyond her previous work. Like Wood, Moreno had recently been getting publicity for her life off the screen. In this case, not all the buzz was welcome: in the spring of 1961, not long after the filming of *West Side Story*, she had attempted suicide over her destructive and mutually obsessive love affair with Marlon Brando. That explanation came many years later; when she was doing interviews and press for *West Side Story*, she declined to answer the inevitable questions posed by reporters. "Life is great," Moreno asserted. "The unhappiness of my past is forgotten and I don't want to talk about it— movies or men."

Even before the New York press had its say, positive reviews had already started coming in from the trade press. *Variety*'s assessment stressed the seriousness of the occasion: "Its stark approach to a raging social problem and realism of unfoldment [sic] may set a pattern for future musical presentations." More straightforward praise came with the *Hollywood Reporter*: "A magnificent show, a milestone in movie

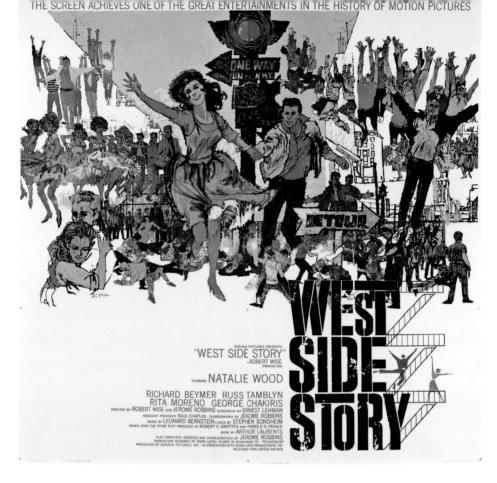

THE SCREEN ACHIEVES ONE OF THE GREAT ENTERTAINMENTS IN THE HISTORY OF MOTION PICTURES

MIRISCH PICTURES PRESENTS
"WEST SIDE STORY"
A ROBERT WISE
PRODUCTION

STARRING NATALIE WOOD

RICHARD BEYMER RUSS TAMBLYN
RITA MORENO GEORGE CHAKIRIS
DIRECTED BY ROBERT WISE AND JEROME ROBBINS SCREENPLAY BY ERNEST LEHMAN
ASSOCIATE PRODUCER SAUL CHAPLIN CHOREOGRAPHY BY JEROME ROBBINS
MUSIC BY LEONARD BERNSTEIN LYRICS BY STEPHEN SONDHEIM
BASED UPON THE STAGE PLAY PRODUCED BY ROBERT E. GRIFFITH AND HAROLD S. PRINCE
BOOK BY ARTHUR LAURENTS
PLAY CONCEIVED, DIRECTED AND CHOREOGRAPHED BY JEROME ROBBINS
PRODUCTION DESIGNED BY BORIS LEVEN FILMED IN PANAVISION 70 TECHNICOLOR
PRESENTED BY MIRISCH PICTURES, INC. IN ASSOCIATION WITH SEVEN ARTS PRODUCTIONS, INC.
RELEASED THRU UNITED ARTISTS

ABOVE: Some of the ad art, especially the posters used overseas, placed the Caroff logo in a more colorfully busy setting.

musicals, a box-office smash. It is so good that superlatives are superfluous." Then, the morning after the premiere, came the reviews from the New York critics, which were mostly in a rapturous key. The *Times*'s stodgy but influential Bosley Crowther used the "M" word—"masterpiece"—and most of the other critics responded similarly: "Gloriously successful" (*Post*); "Must not be missed" (*Herald-Tribune*); "Explosive [if] slightly flawed" (*World-Telegram and Sun*); "Stunning" (*Journal-American*); "Masterful" (*Mirror*); "Thrilling" (*Daily News*). In *Saturday Review*, the

film-savvy Arthur Knight began his piece by recalling his experience, early in 1960, watching Wise and Robbins scouting Manhattan locations. Then he labeled the result of their labor "a triumphant work of art." One of the most thoughtful reviews came in the *New Republic*, from the esteemed Stanley Kauffmann. After enumerating what he felt to be its faults, including inadequate dialog and an insufficient reach for tragedy, he pronounced it "the best film musical ever made." The greatest credit, he said, should go to Robbins, whose work he called "alchemy."

In a later postscript to his review, Kauff-mann wrote about a small but conspicuous portion of the critical reaction to *West Side Story*: the "intelligencia" (his word) tagged it as pretentious pseudo-art with delusions of Shakespeare. This group included Dwight Macdonald, who began his *Esquire* review by looking askance at critics (including Kauff-mann) who had good things to say about the film, then proceeded to take it to task on pretty much every level, including Bern-stein's music. In the *New Yorker*, Brendan Gill complained of the big-movie approach to the material, which he judged to be overbearing, and *Newsweek* found it similarly overblown, "like riding in a powerful car which is stuck in high gear. . . . In the big-screen close-ups, the lovers look like the figures on Mount Rushmore." *Time* complained (like earlier critics of the play), that it attempted to sen-timentalize characters the critic startlingly referred to as "alley rats."

The most famous of the negative reviews, and the most scathing, was recognized as such only in hindsight. In 1962, Pauline Kael was a freelance writer based in the San Fran-cisco Bay Area, reviewing films on a Berkeley radio station and writing occasional pieces for several publications. She eviscerated *West Side Story* on her radio show by using adjectives such as "simpering," "mawkish," and "enfeebled," referring to the Jets and the Sharks as "ballerinas," and terming the whole thing "frenzied hokum." Three years later, her piece resurfaced as one of the more provocative chapters of her first book.

A collection of reviews and essays, *I Lost It at the Movies* instantly established Kael as one of the prickliest and most readable of American film critics and, arguably, the most famous. Her takedown of *West Side Story*, so gleeful that it could be termed performance art, was among the book's most-discussed pieces. Though she might have been loath to admit it, *West Side Story*, was, in a way, the making of Pauline Kael.

Save for Kael and Macdonald, the reviews had been all but unstinting in their praise of Robbins, whose departure from the produc-tion was spoken of, if at all, in tactful tones. *The Hollywood Reporter* took the high road to note that "Rumors of production conflict apparently produced only the healthy stim-ulation of wholesome temperament." Wise's direction also won commendation, in a more restrained key, and Daniel Fapp's cinematog-raphy was singled out again and again. Of the performers, Chakiris and Moreno drew universal praise. Most critics liked Wood as well, and with near-unanimity they declined to comment on her accent. Her dubbed voice was mentioned often, as was that of Beymer, and although the work of the ghost singers had not been publicized, Marni Nix-on's name was sometimes cited. There were good reviews for Tamblyn as well, especially for his acrobatic dancing. Some noted that he seemed a shade clean-cut for a gang leader, a criticism also leveled, repeatedly, at Richard Beymer. Stanley Kauffmann was more blunt: "His earnestness does not compensate for his lack of appeal." It can be added that few other critics in 1961 found Beymer to be an outright liability.

There was nothing, in any case, to dampen the public's enthusiasm. By the end of October, the Rivoli was selling tickets for April and beyond, and the fire was stoked by the November openings in Boston, Philadelphia, and Washington, D.C. Then came a major blast of show-biz excitement. On December 5, Natalie Wood was the centerpiece of one of the most essential of movie rituals: the footprint ceremony in the forecourt of Grauman's Chinese Theatre, in the presence of (as the announcement put it) "Civic and film nobility." The West Coast premiere followed there eight days later, again as a benefit for a commendable cause. This time, the Women's Guild of Cedars-Mount Sinai Hospitals raised $100,000 for its free bed care program. The star quotient was sizable: Lucille Ball, Kirk Douglas, Audrey Hepburn, Jack Benny, Cyd Charisse, Tony Martin, Shirley MacLaine, Jean Simmons, Debbie Reynolds, and many more. Moreno and Chakiris attended together once more, and by now the interest in Wood and Beatty was so intense that *National Geographic* ran a photo of them at the premiere with an article about the character and culture of Los Angeles. For Russ Tamblyn, the highlight of the evening came when someone touched his shoulder and he turned around to find himself looking at Fred Astaire. Upon hearing the master's praise for his dancing, Tamblyn was reduced to dazed babbling. Many of the dancers were there as well, including Yvonne Othon

in a borrowed mink stole. For them, seeing everything they had done projected on the immense Grauman's screen was both thrilling and unnerving. Finally, after all the work, it was all unavoidably, tangibly real, and in some of them there may have flickered the realization that even given their youth, this might be the pinnacle.

Some things in 1961 still hold true today, and one of those is that December marks the beginning of award season. As the various organizations began to announce the year's best, there was no question about the prominence of *West Side Story*. Its main competition came from a pair of grim dramas, Robert Rossen's moody *The Hustler* (1961) and Stanley Kramer's *Judgment at Nuremberg* (1961). Plus, on a plane of slightly less acclaim, *Splendor in the Grass*. It was also the year of Federico Fellini's sensational *La Dolce Vita* (1960), which in most competitions was relegated to the foreign-film category, and Vittorio De Sica's *La ciociara* (*Two Women*) (1960), which put Sophia Loren firmly at the head of most of the year's acting competitions.

It was not, otherwise, one of the more intensive years in terms of "awards bait." *Breakfast at Tiffany's*, *El Cid*, and *The Guns of Navarone* were popular hits, while John Huston's *The Misfits*, Billy Wilder's *One, Two, Three*, and William Wyler's *The Children's Hour* were all judged disappointments from major directors. *Fanny* was an adaptation of a Broadway musical hit with all its songs removed, and otherwise the musical field was light, including Rodgers and Hammerstein's frivolous *Flower Drum Song* and Disney's shiny-but-insubstantial *Babes in Toyland*. There were, in fact, so few musicals released that year that when the Academy was compiling the nominations for Scoring of a Musical Picture, it was found necessary to reach behind the Iron Curtain to nominate Dmitri Shostakovich for arranging the score for the little-seen filmed opera *Khovanschina*.

West Side Story immediately began to lead the awards pack when, on December 28, it was named "Best Picture" by the New York Film Critics Circle. It was also rated one of the year's "Top Ten" by the National Board of Review, which bucked trends by awarding its top prize to the American/German drama *Question 7*. The Golden Globes, presented by the Hollywood Foreign Press Association, were not yet the high-profile bellwether they would become later on. *West Side Story* won in three categories: Best Musical (for which its only competitor was *Flower Drum Song*) and Supporting Actor and Actress nods for Chakiris and Moreno. Wise and Robbins saw the Best Director award go to Stanley Kramer, and Beymer, nominated for "Best Actor, Comedy or Musical," lost to Glenn Ford, in *Pocketful of Miracles*. Both Beymer and Chakiris were also nominees in the Newcomer category, although each had by that time been in movies for over a decade.

TOP: Natalie Wood being "immortalized" at Grauman's Chinese. Costars Moreno, Chakiris, and Tamblyn would follow in those footsteps (and handprints) fifty years later.

BOTTOM: Rita Moreno, still weeping, with Oscar and presenter Rock Hudson

The Academy Awards were next, and it was clear that much of the competition involved two films: *West Side Story* and *Judgment at Nuremberg*, each with eleven nominations. Other contenders included *The Hustler*, with nine nods, followed by seven for *The Guns of Navarone*, and five each for *Breakfast at Tiffany's, The Children's Hour, Fanny*, and *Flower Drum Song*. Both Chakiris and Moreno were nominated in the supporting categories, while Natalie Wood's Best Actress nomination came for *Splendor in the Grass*. All the technical and creative categories received nods, and the nomination for Wise and Robbins marked the first time that two directors were recognized together for one film. Another Academy first gathered as many headlines as the nominations: a week after being cited for his supporting role in *The Hustler*, George C. Scott asked the Academy to withdraw his name from consideration, stating that he did not wish to be part of "a weird beauty or personality contest."

The Oscars came late in those years. This one was April 9, at the Santa Monica Civic Auditorium and televised live on ABC. Although Wood and Beatty caused a photographic frenzy when they arrived, this was long before the era of multiple-hour redcarpet shows, and ABC confined the preliminaries to a couple of quick shots of guests entering the building. The show itself was similarly straightforward, beginning with a performance of "The Star Spangled Banner" by soprano Mary Costa. Johnny Green conducted a special overture, Academy president Wendell Corey explained the voting procedure, and host Bob Hope came out for his monologue. His jokes about current events and the nominees included a predictable dig: "*West Side Story* is about teenagers who carve each other up with switchblades. It's the best musical of the year. [LAUGH] It's the first time I ever saw a gang war and came out whistling the tunes." There were few frills and extras, no large-scale production numbers, and some of the highest-profile nominees, including Judy Garland, Audrey Hepburn, and Sophia Loren, were absent. The banter between Hope and the presenters was brief, the acceptance speeches a matter of a couple of humble sentences, and the musical performances simple and small-scale. (One exception: "Bachelor in Paradise," in which newcomer Ann-Margret attracted a great deal of attention with her sex-kittenish rendition.) One of the few nods to "production value" came with a small Best Costume Design fashion show, in which the young actresses modeling the nominated gowns included one former *West Side* hopeful, Sharon Hugueny.

George Chakiris had led off the awards as a Best Documentary presenter, and only a short time later, he heard his name called. "Wow. I don't believe it," he murmured as presenter Shirley Jones handed him his statuette. "I don't think I'll try and talk too much," he told the audience. "I'll just say thank you, thank you very much." Rita Moreno, something of an upset winner over Judy Garland, was even briefer. In a moment that frequently turns up in montages of Oscar winners, a

ABOVE: **A quartet of winners: Chakiris, Robbins, Wise, and Moreno**

stunned and wide-eyed Moreno exclaimed "I can't be-*lieve* it! Good Lord! I leave you with that." And with that, along with presenter Rock Hudson, she quickly exited.

Again and again, the *West Side Story* team was called up to the podium: Sound, Editing, Scoring of a Musical, Cinematography, Art Direction, Costume Design. All the winners were present, with the exception of Irene Sharaff, who was in Rome working on *Cleopatra*, and Saul Chaplin, in London for the Judy Garland film *I Could Go on Singing* (1963). Some of them thanked both Wise and Robbins, some thanked Wise alone, and to those in the know it was evident that the rift had not entirely healed. "I went to the Academy Awards that night," Mart Crowley remembered, "and believe me, there were two camps: there was the Wise camp and

there was the Robbins. It was pretty frosty out." When Gene Kelly presented him with a special award for "his brilliant achievements in the art of choreography on film," Robbins expressed his gratitude, thanked all those in front of and behind the camera, and did not mention Wise. Later, in consecutive acceptance speeches as Best Director, neither man acknowledged the other. Finally, Wise accepted the Best Picture award and cited Robbins, along with Bernstein, Sondheim, and Laurents, as "the men who are responsible, really, for *West Side Story* being on the screen."

By the end of the evening, there were ten competitive statuettes plus Robbins's special award. Only *Ben-Hur* (1959), in Oscar's thirty-four-year history, had racked up a larger tally of awards, and in later years the only other

ABOVE: A lobby card from Mexico, where the title was translated as "Love Without Barriers"

films to exceed that ten-award total have been *Titanic* (1997) and *The Lord of the Rings: The Return of the King* (2003). The lone nominee who left empty-handed was screenwriter Lehman, a situation he accepted with wry resignation. For neither the first nor last time, Robert Relyea had a colorful story to tell: "It wasn't easy [for Lehman] being the only one to lose. I ran into Ernie in the restroom at the end of the Oscar ceremony. He was at a urinal when another writer stepped up alongside him and blurted out, 'You f—up!'"

Natalie Wood, too, went home without a prize, which caused gossip columnist Hedda Hopper to snipe, in her column, that Wood had been robbed "but at least she got the nicest consolation prize—Warren Beatty." Wood filed for divorce from Robert Wagner later that week. For Robbins, with his mixed feelings about the film itself ("Some of it gets

bogged down," he complained in a letter to a friend) neither the ceremony nor his Oscars meant a great deal. "They're bland like Hollywood," he said of his statuettes, "they're gold and glued over," and he put them in his basement.

If Academy Awards traditionally mean a boost at the box office, the extra adrenaline may not have been necessary in this case. Week by week, the trade press reported a capacity gross in every city, and the road-show engagements lasted so long that the wider openings did not occur, in some places, until 1963. By that time, records were also being set overseas. The foreign premieres—Tokyo, Rio de Janeiro, Paris—were all major events, as was that annual collision of starry and crowned heads, the Royal Film Performance in London, attended by Queen Elizabeth, Princess Margaret, Robert Wise, Richard Beymer, and Russ Tamblyn. In Paris, the premiere at the George V was less regal but more enduring: the engagement lasted 218 weeks, followed by a transfer to another cinema, and then another. The final total of the Parisian first run was a full five years. By 1963, *Variety* reported that *West Side Story* had become number five on the list of all-time highest-grossing films. Eventually, including its theatrical reissue in 1968, the total figure was $44,000,000, which in 2020 dollars is the equivalent of approximately half a billion. "Don't think I'm smart," Natalie Wood once said in an interview. "I was offered a percentage of 'West Side Story' and didn't take it."

Beside the figures connected with the movie itself, astronomical sales were also tallied by the book and the soundtrack. If paperback movie novelizations were a standard commodity, few approached the popularity of this one. Novelist Irving Shulman had already written successfully about juvenile delinquency in *The Amboy Dukes* and *Cry Tough!*, and later on he attracted a great deal of notoriety with a scurrilous biography of Jean Harlow. His *West Side Story* novel, published by Simon & Schuster/Pocket Books, stayed in print long after similar treatments of other movies had vanished, with dozens of printings and, up to the present day, multiple reissues. Following the movie closely, it also added the characters' last names: Tony Wyzek, Maria and Bernardo Nunez, Riff Lorton. Diesel, who had been removed from the film, was reinstated as one of the Jets.

The soundtrack album, released by Colum-bia Records, was in a category all its own, far beyond even such popular soundtracks as *South Pacific*. Made available shortly before the film premiere, the *West Side Story* LP (also available on 4-track stereo reel-to-reel tape) went immediately to the top of the *Billboard* album charts and stayed in the number-one slot for an all-time record of fifty-four weeks.

Like the movie itself, the soundtrack was not without its contentious aspects. As with many previous albums, the ghost singers were as anonymous on the record as they had been on the screen. Worse yet, they had been paid only their initial fees, without any royalties. Having already acquiesced to that with her vocals in *The King and I*, Marni Nixon decided that this time she should fight. Told that there were no remaining royalty points to give her, Nixon and her manager persisted until, finally and generously, Leonard Bernstein gave her a piece of his own percentage. The one joker in this happy-ending deck popped up decades later, when the soundtrack moved to compact disc and continued to sell well. It was then that Nixon discovered that her royalty agreement covered only the sale of LPs, not compact discs. "When records became a thing of the past," Nixon said, "my royalties ceased." Presumably, Nixon (or, now, her estate) was enriched once again with the sales from a 2014 LP re-release of the soundtrack on audiophile vinyl. Betty Wand, who had done some of the singing for Rita Moreno, proved as determined as Nixon, or more so. She sued for royalties and damages, and in 1963 was given an out-of-court settlement.

Following both its road show and continuous showings, the film finally ran its course in about two years. It had attracted interest and excitement and money in greater amounts than those of any previous musical, the album and book sales continued, and occasionally a theater would bring it back for an encore. Otherwise, in that pre-home video time, all that was left was television or, on rare occasions, a theatrical reissue. *West Side Story* warranted the latter treatment, and so it was brought back to theaters in 1968. By that time, the original artwork had given way to brighter graphics, and a new ad campaign cannily tapped into the unrest and youth movements of the later 1960s: "Unlike other classics," the announcer said in the coming-attractions trailer, "*West Side Story* grows younger." Again it was a success, so much so that in some places it out-grossed some of the newer musical films.

Finally, on March 14 and 15, 1972, there was the first television run, which NBC advertised by coming up with what might later be called a meme: three finger snaps, each set to one of the words in the title. Spread over two nights, riddled with commercials, reduced to a pan-and-scan picture that eliminated half the original widescreen image, it still managed to attract a large audience. In New York City, where the ratings share was an immense 61, the telecast was blamed for increased violence in some Manhattan schools, sometimes with attacks accompanied by finger snaps. After that, some of the magic of *West Side Story* seemed to subside: a repeat airing that fall, this time all on one night, brought some of the week's lowest viewing numbers.

The television showings continued over the years, sometimes edited and always with the Panavision image truncated. That pan-and-scan was also an element of the first video release on VHS in 1980. Later, the letterboxed edition on laser disc and then DVD restored the image to its original aspect ratio. The deluxe sets, produced by the Criterion Collection and by MGM, included reminiscences by cast members and even karaoke sing-alongs. Still more editions, around the time of its fiftieth anniversary, brought better sound to Johnny Green's orchestra and high-definition clarity to Daniel Fapp's photography, along with some questionable color remastering that gave the actors' skin tones unpleasantly exaggerated hues of ochre and orange. There were and are also occasional theatrical showings, first on film and later on projected digital video. In a related but separate category are some successful if perhaps curious screenings, in such major venues as the Hollywood Bowl, for which Green's marvelous studio musicians found themselves replaced by a live orchestra. To sum it up cynically, *West Side Story* began as a gold mine, and there will apparently always be fresh, sometimes ingenious ways to tap into its success. Fortunately, one overwhelming and overriding fact remains: it wouldn't have lasted so long if it hadn't had the stuff to begin with.

OPPOSITE: **Poster for the 1968 rerelease**

Unlike other classics "West Side Story" grows younger!

WEST
SIDE
STORY

"BEST
PICTURE!"
Winner of
10 Academy
Awards!

WEST
SIDE
STORY

"WEST SIDE STORY" ROBERT WISE production

NATALIE WOOD

RICHARD BEYMER · RUSS TAMBLYN · RITA MORENO · GEORGE CHAKIRIS · ROBERT WISE and JEROME ROBBINS
ERNEST LEHMAN · JEROME ROBBINS · LEONARD BERNSTEIN · STEPHEN SONDHEIM
ARTHUR LAURENTS · JEROME ROBBINS

United Artists

CHAPTER SEVEN

ONCE AND FOR ALL: MORTALITY AND IMMORTALITY

—

"So how do you follow West Side Story?"

JOANNE MIYA [NOBUKO MIYAMOTO]
(Francisca)

ABOVE: Natalie Wood (in her "Let Me Entertain You" costume) on the set of *Gypsy* (1962) with assistant and friend Mart Crowley

PAGE 162: Debbie Allen (center) as Anita in the 1980 Broadway revival.

I**N ITS REVIEW, *NEWSWEEK* HAD** compared the close-ups of Tony and Maria to Mount Rushmore. By doing this, it was making, however unintentionally, an important point: *West Side Story* was indeed a kind of monument. For many of those associated with it, there would seldom again be work that arduous, that intense, that collaborative, that rewarding. Perhaps, even, that transcendent. For many, it had been a once-in-a-lifetime accomplishment, and may possibly, for some, have been *the* high point. Russ Tamblyn realized this later on: "[I wish] someone had come up to me at the time and said, 'You better appreciate this, because it'll be the highest time in your life, you'll probably

never top this.' I'm sure I'll go to my grave and it'll say 'Russ Tamblyn from *West Side Story.*'"

It stood alone, and there would be no sequels to show Maria moving on or the Jets and the Sharks resuming their hostilities. There were, however, some foreseeable repercussions, from the film as well as the show. Perhaps that was most evident on Broadway, where it could translate as relevance of subject matter, focus of storytelling, and pertinence of music and dance. "Relevance," in this case, did not necessarily refer to ripped-from-the-headlines immediacy. Instead, it could come from a place as unexpected as the memoir of a notorious celebrity. So it was, in between the stage and film versions of *West Side Story*, that three of the show's creators collaborated on a musical about the empress of stripteasers, Gypsy Rose Lee. In 1959, Jerome Robbins directed and choreographed *Gypsy*, with a book by Arthur Laurents and lyrics by Stephen Sondheim. If this "musical fable" about Lee and her mother lacked its predecessor's perceived gravitas, and if it did not employ dance in the same intrinsic fashion, it was ultimately every bit as acute dramatically. In 1959, its resonance was perhaps camouflaged by the show-biz flash of both its source and its star performer, Ethel Merman. It took time, decades of it, for *Gypsy* to emerge as every bit as worthy and consequential as *West Side Story*—an equally seminal musical play, a companion piece even, albeit in a vastly different key.

It was as much through coincidence as anything that the film version of *Gypsy* was one of the first two major musicals released after *West Side Story*. Both of them were based on hit shows, both were reasonably faithful, and both were products of a slowly fading studio system, in this case Warner Bros. *The Music Man* was first, bustling and capably assembled and, happily, preserving the dynamic stage performance of Robert Preston. *Gypsy* was not as acclaimed, nor quite as popular, due partly to resentment that Ethel Merman had been passed over in favor of Rosalind Russell. Natalie Wood, cast as the young Gypsy Rose Lee, was once again beset by insecurity during production, inevitably worrying (needlessly, this time) that her singing might be replaced by that of a double. Yet, perhaps more than

with Maria, Wood identified with the role: like Lee, she had started young in show business under the guidance of an ambitious, often overbearing mother. In the penultimate scene of the daughter telling off her mother, Wood's conviction was impossible to miss.

Neither *Gypsy* nor *The Music Man* were part of the road-show film phenomenon, which over the next few years was given over to spectacles, not musicals: *The Longest Day* (1962), *Lawrence of Arabia, How the West Was Won* (1962), and the ultimate behemoth, *Cleopatra*. It was not until October of 1964 that another road-show musical had an impact comparable to *West Side Story*. *My Fair Lady*, also from Warner Bros., was an immensely expensive undertaking that cast a box-office name, Audrey Hepburn, in place of the (then) lesser known Julie Andrews. Hepburn recorded her own vocal tracks, then later learned to her disappointment that Marni Nixon was going to overdub them. This time, there was no effort to keep the news a secret, though once again Nixon was not given credit on the soundtrack album. The production took few risks, won multiple Academy Awards and, more than *West Side Story*, was as preordained a hit as could be imagined; the prestige and pedigree of *My Fair Lady* might have brought success to any film version short of a total catastrophe.

A few months after *My Fair Lady* opened, the next big road-show musical premiered at the Rivoli Theatre. More than big, as produced and directed by Robert Wise, the *biggest*. On Broadway, *The Sound of Music* had been as far removed from *West Side Story* as it was possible to be. On film, with Wise reunited with Ernest Lehman and Saul Chaplin, it became a success like no other, a mammoth crowd-pleaser expertly calibrated to give the most entertainment to the greatest possible number of spectators. It also gave Wise the opportunity to quote *West Side Story*. In the opening scene, before Julie Andrews launched into the title song, Wise began his film, once again, with spellbinding aerial shots. Only now, instead of ominous urban vistas, they were views of castles and gorgeous countrysides. *The Sound of Music*, for which Wise won two more Oscars, became for a while the top-grossing movie of all time. This time, it was followed by many imitators and more road-show musicals, a few of which were successful and quite a few which were not. Wise himself had a major failure with his third musical, *Star!* (1968), and after the early 1970s, the road-show era was over. The big musicals that came later, such as *Grease* and *The Wiz* (both 1978), were destined to play to different kinds of moviegoers in a greatly changed world.

Unlike road-show musicals, the people who made *West Side Story* did keep going. Each of them had a different "Then what happened?" story, and many did not follow along the paths that might have been anticipated. Russ Tamblyn, for one, found few further opportunities equal to that of playing Riff. He made more films, including Robert Wise's *The Haunting* (1963), did a fair amount of television work, and turned down the lead role in *Gilligan's Island*. The nadir

came in 1969, when something called *Satan's Sadists* announced that it featured "His greatest role since *West Side Story*." Disillusioned with the acting profession, Tamblyn turned to other kinds of art—collages, mixed media, and performances pieces. Eventually, as an accomplished artist, he would alternate shows and exhibits with occasional film and television appearances, and he also directed and choreographed Neil Young's rock opera *Greendale*. In 1989, he played what truly was his greatest role since Riff: the eccentric countercultural psychiatrist Dr. Lawrence Jacoby in *Twin Peaks*, which he repeated when the cult show returned to television in 2017. "In entertainment," Tamblyn has said, "your function is to make the audience's head spin . . . in art, your function is to make your own head spin."

George Chakiris and Richard Beymer also eventually found fulfilling work outside the realm of performing. After winning the Academy Award, Chakiris appeared in a big-scale soap opera, *Diamond Head* (1963); then, opposite Yul Brynner, he portrayed a Mayan ruler in a critical and financial calamity of a spectacle called *Kings of the Sun* (1963). Jacques Demy's *The Young Girls of Rochefort* (1967) gave him the opportunity to sing and dance once again, while he also recorded several albums and performed in Las Vegas. Like Russ Tamblyn, he starred in a 1969 film of numbing awfulness: his was the Lana-Turner-on-LSD melodrama *The Big Cube*, which a later critic termed "the kind of movie that serves only to remind us how

ABOVE: George Chakiris (with Marti Stevens) in the national tour of Stephen Sondheim's *Company* (1971)

low a studio could stoop." On television, he acted in shows ranging from *The Partridge Family* to *Medical Center* in the 1970s, with later recurring roles on the series *Dallas* and *Superboy*. There was also a good deal of stage work, including the national tour of *Company* and a Los Angeles revival of *The King and I*. By the early twenty-first century, he had stopped performing and turned his focus to making and marketing his own line of silver jewelry, the George Chakiris Collections.

Beymer was part of the ensemble cast of *The Longest Day* and starred in three unsuccessful films: *Five Finger Exercise* (1962), *Hemingway's Adventures of a Young Man* (1962), and *The Stripper* (1963). His dissatisfaction with the movie business led him to study for a while at the Actors Studio and, in 1964, make a trip to Mississippi

to photograph and eventually participate in the Freedom Summer drive to register minority voters. The latter experience was for him far more fulfilling than the television work that occasionally popped up, not to mention another 1969 release of less-than-sterling quality: *Scream Free!* (1969), also known as *Free Grass*, in which he starred alongside Russ Tamblyn and was paired with Natalie Wood's sister Lana. "The Stars of *West Side Story* together again!" the ads screamed, hopefully. After this, he turned to photography and filmmaking and left California. He resumed his acting career in 1984 with the television series *Paper Dolls* and later appeared on *Dallas, Moonlighting,* and *Murder, She Wrote*. Like Russ Tamblyn, he enjoyed something of a career revival in *Twin Peaks*, playing the sinister tycoon Benjamin Horne, in the original series and again

NOW! THE STARS OF WEST SIDE STORY TOGETHER AGAIN!

HOLLYWOOD STAR PICTURES presents

FREE GRASS

LOVE AND VIOLENCE FORM A MIND-BLOWING TRIP!!!

BEST ADULT FILM OF THE YEAR! *ADAM* FILM QUARTERLY

FILMED IN EASTMAN COLOR

starring RICHARD BEYMER • LANA WOOD • RUSS TAMBLYN • JOEL DEE McCREA • LINDSAY CROSBY • CASEY KASEM
Produced by JOHN LAWRENCE • Executive Producer ARTHUR N. GILBERT • Directed by BILL BRAME
Screenplay by JAMES GORDON WHITE and JOHN LAWRENCE • Musical Score by SIDEWALK PRODUCTIONS, INC.
A MAURICE SMITH-RAY DORN-LYNN STEED PRODUCTION.

69/356

in its 2017 return. While continuing to take photographs and work on documentary and experimental films, he wrote and published an idiosyncratic "fictionalized autobiography," *Imposter*. Unlike his costars, he has appeared only rarely at events connected with *West Side Story*. "In my mind," he once said in an interview, "I never left the movies. I just made other kinds of movies."

Robert Wise had been especially enthusiastic about the young actor he cast as the oblivious social worker Glad Hand, and after that role John Astin began to appear virtually nonstop in dozens of television shows and films. He was particularly memorable as Doris Day's would-be seducer in *That Touch of Mink* (1962), and in 1964 he achieved TV immortality as the jauntily macabre patriarch of *The Addams Family*. Through the subsequent decades, appearing on-screen, doing voiceovers, and eventually as an acting teacher, Astin worked steadily. He even won an Academy Award nomination for directing the short film *Prelude* (1968). If the specter of Gomez Addams never abandoned him completely, it was at least a spirit with a cheerful and benevolent aura that was, to be sure, far more clued-in than Glad Hand.

For the biggest name in *West Side Story*, the journey ended far too soon. After her successes in *Splendor in the Grass, West Side Story*, and *Gypsy*, Natalie Wood received a third Oscar nomination for *Love with the Proper Stranger* (1963). Two comedies, *Sex*

OPPOSITE: Tony, Riff, and "Maria's sister," together again, in a mind-blowing trip in 1969

and the Single Girl (1964) and *The Great Race* (1965), were followed by two ambitious disappointments, *Inside Daisy Clover* (1965) and *This Property Is Condemned* (1966). After turning down the opportunity to star opposite former beau Warren Beatty in *Bonnie and Clyde* (1967), she triumphed in a cutting-edge hit, *Bob & Carol & Ted & Alice* (1969). Wood then took a hiatus to focus on her personal life. Two weddings and two daughters later, she resumed her career in films like *Meteor* (1979) and on television in movies such as *The Cracker Factory* (1979) and the miniseries *From Here to Eternity* (1979). If the white-hot flash of 1961 had dimmed somewhat, she continued to radiate a distinctive and quite endearing kind of star luster. The enormous outpouring of public grief after her shocking accidental death in 1981 was both genuine and deeply felt.

While working on *Splendor in the Grass*, Natalie Wood had met a young writer and assistant named Mart Crowley, and by the end of production they had bonded so strongly that she asked him to go back to Los Angeles to serve as her secretary and companion. Nearly immediately, Crowley was plunged into the off-screen drama that was the making of *West Side Story*. Part of that drama involved Howard Jeffrey, Jerome Robbins's assistant, with whom both Wood and Crowley developed a close friendship. Over the next few years, Wood encouraged Crowley's writing and, when he was beset by doubt and demons, she paid for his psychoanalysis. Eventually, he completed a play he called *The Boys in the Band*, which was a smash hit off-Broadway in 1968. He had based the characters on a number of his friends, and the key role of Harold was modeled in large part on Howard Jeffrey. Both Jeffrey and Crowley remained close friends with Wood and, long after her death, with her daughter Natasha. *The Boys in the Band* finally made its Broadway debut in a fiftieth anniversary production, for which Crowley received a Tony Award for Best Revival of a Play.

The *West Side Story* dancers, so bonded and committed—if occasionally anarchic—during the months of rehearsal and filming, found their subsequent careers keeping them in dance for a time, then often leading to some unexpected places. Few of them approached their careers with more exuberance than David Winters, Baby John on the stage and A-Rab in the film. By 1964, at the age of twenty-four, he had begun to stage the dances of films such as *Viva Las Vegas* (1964) and *Billie* (1965), and was soon producing and sometimes directing TV specials for Lucille Ball, Ann-Margret, Raquel Welch, Nancy Sinatra, and Sonny and Cher. Later, he choreographed Barbra Streisand's *A Star Is Born* (1976), directed the Alice Cooper concert film *Welcome to My Nightmare* (1975), and produced dozens of films for his own company, West Side Studios. By the time of his death in 2019, he had amassed over two hundred film and television credits.

His fellow Jet (A-Rab, then Action) Tony Mordente also moved behind the camera, first as a choreographer and then as one of television's busiest directors. Beginning in the mid-1970s and continuing for nearly three decades, Mordente's name would be in the credits of literally hundreds of sitcoms, mystery dramas, and action series. Gus Trikonis, Indio the Shark, was nearly as prolific. First he directed feature films with titles like *The Swinging Barmaids* (1975) and *Moonshine County Express* (1977). Then, on television, there followed a long procession of movies and numerous episodes of such series as *Baywatch* and *Beauty and the Beast*.

A few of the Jets remained closer to their dance roots. Eliot Feld, who replaced Winters as Baby John on Broadway and repeated the role on film, joined the American Ballet Theatre at age twenty-one and, four years later, formed his own dance company. As the leader of the Feld Ballet, and as a choreographer, teacher, and director, he became one of the most prominent and respected figures in American dance. Tommy Abbott, Gee-Tar, continued to work with Robbins as both a dancer and, for *Fiddler on the Roof*, assistant choreographer. He staged the dances for revivals of both *West Side Story* and *Fiddler*, and also for *Fiddler*'s film adaptation in 1971. The latter assignment became his because, as executive producer Walter Mirisch discreetly put it, "This time the services of Jerome Robbins were not part of the arrangement."

Anthony "Scooter" Teague (Big Deal) alternated between dancing on film and on the stage, including two national tours of *A*

Chorus Line and the Broadway production of *No, No, Nanette*. Tucker Smith, a replacement Riff on Broadway and Ice in the movie, also worked in film, television, and on the stage; his roles grew smaller because, as historian David Ehrenstein observed, "he wasn't inclined to be closeted" during a time when few performers were openly gay. Harvey Hohnecker changed his name to Harvey Evans and, over the next forty years and more, was one of the busiest and most likable actors in musical theater, including such shows as *Hello, Dolly!*, *Follies*, and *La Cage aux Folles*. For Robert Banas, more film work as a dancer—*Bye Bye Birdie* (1963), *The Unsinkable Molly Brown* (1964), *Mary Poppins* (1964)—was followed by years as a choreographer and teacher. Then, in a complete change, he turned to "outside" work, literally: landscaping and gardening. (His motto: "Don't forget to smell the roses!") David Bean also left the profession, eventually operating a farm and a succession of retail businesses, while Bert Michaels's second career came as a producer of private and corporate events, including numerous movie premieres.

Many of the former Sharks fared comparably—dance first, then branching out. Eddie Verso, Baby John in the London production and the movie's Juano, stayed closer to dance than anyone else in the cast except Eliot Feld. He worked for Jerome Robbins in the Ballets: U.S.A. company, then became a principal dancer with the American Ballet Theatre and the Joffrey Ballet. Later, he

founded his own company, Dance Center of NJ, and restaged some of Robbins's works on behalf of the Robbins Foundation. Jay Norman (Juano on stage, Pepe on film) had earlier been part of Robbins's Ballets: U.S.A. and returned to the company after the film, along with Robert Thompson, who had played Luis. Larry Roquemore, a replacement Gee-Tar in the show and Rocco in the movie, returned to Broadway to dance in such shows as *Anyone Can Whistle* and *Hallelujah, Baby!* Jaime Rogers (Loco) served as a choreographer for *Fame*, *The Sonny and Cher Show*, and other TV series, while Andre Tayir (Chile) did similar work with *Shindig!* and a number of TV specials, as well as the film *Star Trek III: The Search for Spock* (1984). Nick Covacevich, later Nick Navarro (Toro) staged the dances for numerous shows in Las Vegas and elsewhere. Jose De Vega (Chino), continued to act in film and on television for the better part of three decades, while Rudy Del Campo (Del Campo) eventually left show business completely to work as a restaurateur.

Most of the women, too, stayed with dancing before finding other paths. Yvonne Othon, now Yvonne Wilder, played Anita in countless productions and touring companies of *West Side Story* and became half of the comedy duo Colvin and Wilder. Later she performed in dozens of sitcoms and dramas, including *Full House,* as Uncle Jesse's mother, and *Archie Bunker's Place,* as Archie's post–Edith Bunker romantic interest. Eventually, as with Tamblyn and Gus

Trikonis, she channeled her creativity in the direction of fine art—watercolors, oils, and sculpture. Two other Shark women, Suzie Kaye and Linda Dangcil, also worked extensively in television, the latter playing Sister Ana in *The Flying Nun*. Maria Jimenez Henley (Teresita) danced in more films, including *Thoroughly Modern Millie* (1967), in which she performed in one number as her "normal" self and in another as an eighty-year-old grandmother. Later, she would be stage manager for *Saved by the Bell* and other TV series, and later still began yet another career, as a writer.

Gina Trikonis danced and choreographed in film, television, and nightclubs before moving on to a long second career in television as a costume supervisor. Joanne Miya (Nobuko Miyamoto) performed for a while and eventually founded Great Leap, a Los Angeles–based organization which, as its mission statement declares, "uses art as both performance and creative practice to deepen relations among people of diverse cultures and faiths." Susan Oakes (Anybodys) stopped performing entirely, and Carole D'Andrea, Velma on stage and on film, opted for temporary retirement, marriage to Broadway star Robert Morse, and motherhood. She returned as a teacher, coach, and director, in New York, Europe, and, eventually Los Angeles, leading classes in both acting and singing for countless performers.

For most of the crew members, *West Side Story* was less a seminal experience than a rewarding job. Irene Sharaff and Boris Leven continued to work on large productions, often musicals, and Daniel Fapp photographed stars like Elvis Presley and Doris Day until he retired in 1969. Having survived his stint as "headmaster" to the Jets and the Sharks, Robert Relyea was assistant director or production manager for several more films before forming a partnership with Steve McQueen. He served as executive producer of *Bullitt* (1968) and *Le Mans* (1971), after which he was a producer of such films as *The Deer Hunter* (1978) and *Last Action Hero* (1993). In the 1990s, he became executive vice president, then president, of worldwide production for MGM/United Artists. Saul Chaplin, following the smash of *The Sound of Music*, worked on two further roadshow musicals that did far less well: Wise's *Star!* and *Man of La Mancha*. Following *That's Entertainment, Part 2*, in 1976, Chaplin left film because the movie musical was in a state he described in his memoirs as "lamentable." Johnny Green remained in film until the end of the 1960s and won his fifth Academy Award for *Oliver!* (1968). Of the two musical arrangers, Irwin Kostal stayed in film (*Mary Poppins, The Sound of Music, Bedknobs and Broomsticks* [1971]), while Sid Ramin's later work included (along with much else), some of the most popular TV commercial jingles of the 1960s and the indelible theme song for *The Patty Duke Show*.

Having helped revolutionize film production, the Mirisch Company continued to be responsible for hits for decades more. These included *The Pink Panther* (1963), *In the Heat* of the Night (1967), *The Thomas Crown Affair* (1968), and *Fiddler on the Roof*. (Just for the sake of variety, it can be noted that the Mirisch roster also included the occasional misstep like *Kings of the Sun*.) The most high-profile of the Mirisch brothers, Walter, served four terms as president of the Motion Picture Academy, received countless awards and citations, and maintained an active interest in film well into the twenty-first century. In 2016, in the middle of his tenth decade, he was credited as an executive producer of the Denzel Washington remake of a much earlier Mirisch hit, *The Magnificent Seven*. Upbeat and astute, Walter Mirisch managed to summarize his work ethic with the title of his autobiography: *I Thought We Were Making Movies, Not History*.

For Jerome Robbins, the cinematic incarnation of *West Side Story* was mainly something to acknowledge, then move beyond. "The thing is in the past," he told a reporter, adding that "I was used as a patsy for some people without enough experience in the problems of filming musicals." After more experiences in musical and straight theater, most successfully *Fiddler on the Roof*, he left Broadway to put his focus completely on dance. With the New York City Ballet as his home base, he created scores of new works that established him, alongside George Balanchine, as one of the world's masters. Later, he returned to musical theater in a retrospective sense, supervising restagings of *West Side Story* and *Fiddler on the Roof* and in 1989 directing the long-running compendium *Jerome Robbins' Broadway*, for which he won his fifth Tony Award. Until his death in 1998,

he went on inspiring and sometimes terrifying new generations of dancers, his acknowledged genius generally excusing his brilliant knack for straying outside the boundaries of acceptable conduct.

As codirector of *West Side Story*, Robert Wise had not been given praise on the level showered upon Robbins. *The Sound of Music*, however, was entirely his, and he had another success with *The Sand Pebbles* (1966). Then followed the major disappointment of *Star!*, whose cost had been that of *West Side Story* and *The Sound of Music* combined. *Star!* had the misfortune to open just after another musical biopic, *Funny Girl* (1968), and the audiences who thronged to see Barbra Streisand as a lovelorn Fanny Brice were far less interested in seeing Julie Andrews playing Gertrude Lawrence, who was depicted as self-absorbed and not particularly likable. Wise, who vigorously defended *Star!* in later years, moved on to a mixed bag of projects: *The Andromeda Strain* (1971), *The Hindenburg* (1975), *Star Trek: The Motion Picture* (1979). Most were moderate successes at best, without the excitement of *West Side Story* or the invincibility of *The Sound of Music*. After *Star Trek*, Wise spent nearly a decade on hiatus, after which he returned to both filmmaking and, twenty-seven years after the fact, to *West Side Story*.

Wise's *Rooftops* (1989) was the tale of racially mixed street gangs living in improvised shacks atop some abandoned Manhattan tenements. They express themselves in a kind of ritualized rumble-through-dance while battling crack dealers and, occasionally, each other. A Caucasian hero falls in love with a Hispanic heroine whose brother is a drug lord, and there ensue several deaths, more dancing, and a reasonably happy ending. The soundtrack featured songs by the Eurhythmics, Trouble Funk, and Kisses from the Kremlin, and much of John Carrafa's choreography was based on the Brazilian dance form *capoeira*. For Wise, then in his midseventies, it was an incongruous and rather poignant attempt to recapture some past glory and find a place on the cutting edge. "Wise has worn many hats during his career and won many awards," the *Washington Post* noted, "but the last thing anybody would call him is 'homeboy.'" A few charitable critics, Roger Ebert among them, were able to pick out fleeting good moments and, as with many late failures from reputable artists, *Rooftops* came and went with undue rapidity. Wise directed one more film, for television, and until his death in 2005 spent a good deal of time attending retrospectives, accepting plaudits, and giving interviews. Ever a gracious raconteur, soft-spoken, approachable, and eternally positive, he was happy to discuss *West Side Story* by sharing his versions of some familiar stories: his decision to shoot on location and open with an aerial montage, his casting Natalie Wood while seeing her in a test with Warren Beatty, and, as recounted with impressive tact, the firing of Jerome Robbins.

One of the chief reasons *Rooftops* seemed so dim was that, by the time it opened, *West Side Story* was on the highest shelf of American classics. If a good portion of this esteem came from the show's impact and worth, the film played an incalculable role as well, perhaps even a dominant one. Had the movie not been made or not been made well, there would have been other productions of the show but, as previously noted, this was a case of love for a movie going beyond that given to the original. It does not happen often. The successful film versions of *Oklahoma!* or *Guys and Dolls* (1955), to name two, did not displace the regard people had for those shows on the stage. People loved *The King and I* on the screen as they had on Broadway and yet they stayed separate, while the huge success of the movie of *South Pacific* came almost solely because the show itself was so good. *West Side Story* was a different matter entirely: its magic lay in the exciting way the work itself and the filmmaking complemented each other. The movie expanded on the show while respecting it and, as a result, both were raised up. That mutual enhancement, the interrelation between the show and the movie, benefited both works. Even for people who understood that Maria and Tony were not singing for themselves, or took issue with something or other, the movie resonated so powerfully that in a way, for millions, it *became* the show.

Curiously and perhaps coincidentally, the other looming example of this "movie overtaking the show" phenomenon was that second product from the Robert Wise musical workshop, *The Sound of Music*. On

ABOVE: Robert Wise directing Jason Gedrick in *Rooftops* (1989).

Broadway, the show had been judged quite conventional, which did not keep it from running twice as long as *West Side Story*. On film, with changes to its script and songs, plus the presence of Julie Andrews and location photography, it became more direct, more dynamic, more communicative. With much of the firm craft that Wise had brought to *West Side Story*, if without such challenging immediacy, it outstripped the show almost right away. Subsequent stage productions of *The Sound of Music* must now operate, for better or worse, in the film's shadow, and (as is also the case with *Grease*) sometimes change the original work to make it conform closer to a film, which so many have seen and adore.

After the release of *West Side Story*, and throughout the 1960s and '70s, there were numerous regional and touring productions of the show in America and abroad. They suffered from comparison with the Robbins staging captured on film, yet the work itself and the film both maintained their hold on the public's imagination. In 1980, when Robbins supervised a moderately successful Broadway revival, most critics felt that it was not so much dynamic as merely dutiful, with only Debbie Allen's Anita having much vibrancy. Even for those who decried the things the movie may not have gotten completely right, it was clearly more exciting than revival attempts.

By the next time the show appeared on Broadway, in 2009, much had changed—in musical theater, film, and the outside world. Directed by the ninety-one-year-old Arthur Laurents, with the original Robbins dances faithfully reproduced, it was the same *West Side Story* . . . only different. In a much-publicized bow to cultural authenticity, many

ABOVE: Turner Classic Movies host Robert Osborne with Marni Nixon, George Chakiris, and Walter Mirisch at the 2011 TCM Classic Film Festival in Hollywood

of the words spoken and sung by the Puerto Rican characters were translated into Spanish by Lin-Manuel Miranda. "I Feel Pretty" was now "Siento Hermosa" and "A Boy Like That" became "Un Hombre Asi," and the attention given to these changes tended to overshadow the other factors, pro and con, of the production. Except for the language, and a greater number of Hispanic cast members, it was the show much as before, as opposed to the drastic reimagining given to other shows such as *Cabaret* in 1998 and, in 2019, *Oklahoma!* The New York critics, in generally favorable notices, sometimes made passing (occasionally sneering) reference to the film, but if this new revival had some ethnic credibility that had been missing in 1961, it was not seen as significantly different, let alone better. Once again, the Anita, played by Karen Olivo, captured the best reviews (and a Tony Award), and the show ran a few performances longer

than the original production. By that time, Laurents and the producers had decided that many of the Spanish words lacked the necessary impact for most audiences, and had them put back into their original English.

The "reimagining" not present in 2009 would arrive, emphatically so, with yet another revival in 2020. In the tradition of many drastic reconceptions, this one had a creative team with a strongly European avant-garde flavor: director Ivo van Hove, choreographer Anne Teresa De Keersmaeker, and designer Jan Versweyveld. The production, it was reported, would mark the first time that Broadway would witness a *West Side Story* not conceived and choreographed by Jerome Robbins. With Van Hove's trademark minimalist style, along with De Keersmaeker's signature angular, slashing choreography, this production became a topic of discussion and controversy long before it even opened. In doing so, it attracted a great deal of attention to itself, to the show's enduring popularity, and to the movie. (Make that, in 2020, "movies.")

However, it is interpreted or reconceived, on stage or on film, *West Side Story* will still, of necessity, stay essentially the same. It is a musical tragedy of rare honesty—timeless in many ways—bold, brilliant, astonishing, and imperfect. Might some find it dated, naïve, or too familiar? For those disposed to take that position, the characters might seem formulaic, the Shakespearean allusions forced, the cultural misconceptions prominent. These are not invalid observations, yet they cannot preclude or deny the invincible spell that the movie casts so powerfully. Even when minimized to home video and parodied to death, it endures, and stays remarkably fresh. If it is not, as Stanley Kauffmann had called it, "The best film musical ever made," it remains one of the most special, singular, and loved. Unlike many other Oscar winners, it has stayed perpetually vibrant, nostalgic in a good way, bold in degrees that overcome its compromises. Over the years, as anniversaries came around and newly remastered versions were released, *West Side Story* seemed to ratify itself as one of the rare classics that could keep going and be worth celebrating. The cast members, both leads and dancers, would be called on to attend screenings, give interviews, reminisce, and offer the occasional nugget of insight, hindsight, or gossip. To celebrate the release of a new Blu-Ray version in 2011, *West Side Story* returned to

Grauman's Chinese for a fiftieth anniversary screening. There, trim and smiling in their later seventies, the former Riff, Anita, and Bernardo added their hand- and footprints to those of Natalie Wood in the theater's forecourt.

Among all the cast members, it was Rita Moreno who traveled what was possibly the longest and most conspicuous post–*West Side Story* career path. At first, it all seemed to be a crushing disappointment for her. There was virtually no Oscar boost, no choice of roles, and only more opportunities to play a spitfire (a word she detested) once again. One film (*Cry of Battle* [1963], which she later described as "really crappy"), a few guest spots on television, and a worthy Broadway flop (*The Sign in Sidney Brustein's Window*) were the sum of her acting career for seven years. Private life proved more rewarding, including a marriage to cardiologist Leonard Gordon and a daughter. Finally, there came work that seemed to be worth the effort: a riveting cameo as a sex worker in *Carnal Knowledge* (1971), a long and much-applauded stint on the children's PBS series *The Electric Company,* and a return to Broadway in Terrence McNally's comedy *The Ritz*. As Googie Gomez, a lounge performer of vast ambition and zero talent, Moreno seized triumphantly on the opportunity to spoof all the stereotyped roles that had hindered her for so many years. Her performance in *The Ritz* brought her a Tony Award, and she promptly became one of the first people to win the show business quadruple crown,

later known as the EGOT: Emmy (two of them), Grammy (for the *Electric Company* album), Oscar, and Tony. Into her sixties and seventies she performed steadily and, it seemed, tirelessly, proving by example that talent and determination could overcome demeaning concepts of age, sex, and ethnicity.

If her roles were sometimes routine, Moreno's professionalism and commitment never were, and fortunately there were some worthy opportunities. In the HBO series *Oz*, playing a sternly compassionate nun serving in a grim prison facility, she seemed a million miles away from Anita or her other earlier roles. Later, she was cast hilariously against type as a Jewish mother in the sitcom *Happily Divorced*, and around that same time the body-of-work awards began to roll in: the Presidential Medal of Freedom, the National Medal of Arts, the Screen Actors Guild Lifetime Achievement Award, the Kennedy Center Honors, and a Peabody Career Achievement Award. She wrote a tell-much autobiography, starred onstage in a one-woman show, and then kept going. At the age of eighty-five, playing the grandmother in an updated version of the oldie *One Day at a Time*, she was again a delight and, with her vivacity and comic timing, such a wonder that the *New York Times* could only salute her as "the brightest star in our solar system." After that, there was a rather stunning case of an outstanding career taking an old-yet-new turn.

In 1960, Rita Moreno had been one of the first actors to audition for *West Side Story*, returning ceaselessly for further readings, dance auditions, and screen tests until the final word came that she had been cast. Unlike other "hot-tempered" characters she had been playing for a decade, the role of Anita had substance and a degree of authenticity. In later years, Moreno recounted her experiences on the film with clear-eyed candor: the hard work involved in rehearsing and shooting the dances, the blistering perfectionism of Jerome Robbins, the demeaning "one color fits all" makeup worn by all those playing Puerto Ricans, the disappointment with the dubbed voice given her for "A Boy Like That," the pain of filming that horrifying scene of Anita being mauled by the Jets, and the elation in the Puerto Rican community when she won her Oscar. Also, the dispiriting aftermath, when there were few opportunities any better than what there had been before Anita. While that last part changed, Anita would remain a high point and landmark in a career spanning eight decades. Much had happened since then in her life and career, yet somehow the conviction of that performance retained a distinct glow. Much of it was due to how good Moreno had been in the role, and a fair amount also had to do with the unique way, over the following decades, she had endured and kept rising to new challenges. Then, somewhat unexpectedly, *West Side Story* beckoned once again.

OPPOSITE: Rita Moreno in *One Day at a Time* (2017)

CHAPTER EIGHT
A NEW WAY:
THE 2020 VERSION

—

"You want to talk about full circle, huh? It's crazy."
RITA MORENO
(Anita in 1961, Valentina in 2020)

ABOVE: Ansel Elgort as Tony and Rachel Zegler as Maria, flanked by Mike Faist (Riff) and David Alvarez (Bernardo) in Steven Spielberg's 2020 remake of *West Side Story*

PAGE 191: Maria, 1960

ONE WAY OR ANOTHER, THE NEWS had been circulating for years: Steven Spielberg was contemplating a remake of *West Side Story*. At points it seemed close to happening then, as with many extravagant rumors, it receded. Finally, in 2018, there was official word. Spielberg would be directing a new Twentieth Century Fox production of *West Side Story*, with prize-winning playwright Tony Kushner writing the screenplay and the eminent conductor Gustavo Dudamel leading the musical forces. Very shortly after that, it began to seem like 1960 all over again: wild casting rumors, all manner of speculation, thousands of potential Jets and Sharks being considered and tested. Eventually, news began to trickle out about the cast. Ansel Elgort would be Tony, with Mike Faist as Riff, Ariana DeBose as Anita, and David Alvarez as Bernardo. Just as it had in 1960, the announce-

ment for Maria came last. Seventeen-year-old Rachel Zegler, born in New Jersey to a Polish father and Colombian mother, had already attracted attention on Twitter when her performance of "Shallow," the Lady Gaga song from *A Star Is Born* (2018), hit over seven million views.

Also in the cast announcements was the most specific possible link to the original. Rita Moreno would serve as an executive producer and play a new variant of an old role: Doc, the kindly candy-store owner, was now Moreno's Valentina, Doc's widow. The production would be set in the show's original time period, with shooting locations selected in Manhattan, Brooklyn, and New Jersey. Filming began in the summer of 2019, with a release date set for December of 2020. This heady news was greeted with reactions spanning as wide a spectrum as one might expect—excitement, suspicion, exasperation, and a great deal of curiosity. Why Spielberg, why now, why a remake of an acknowledged classic?

Why, indeed. There are countless answers, since the notion of remaking a film has been an imperative since the dawn of movies. Before television and home video, most films finished their initial runs and were then effectively dead. A few big movies—*Gone With the Wind*, Disney features, *King Kong* (1933)— might be brought back, and some others, if they were lucky, could get a brief revival. Remakes, then, could be a way of bringing back a favorite story while keeping the studio assembly line humming, be it with *Dr. Jekyll and Mr. Hyde, Les Misérables*, or *Show Boat*. The success rate varied widely. MGM scored hugely with a new *Ben-Hur* and not happily with the second *Mutiny on the Bounty.* Alfred Hitchcock fared well when he remade *The Man Who Knew Too Much* (1956), as did Cecil B. DeMille with *The Ten Commandments* (1956), and producer Ross Hunter's updated versions of *Magnificent Obsession* (1954) and *Imitation of Life* (1959) were massive successes. *The Blue Angel* (1959), *Stagecoach* (1966), and *Psycho* (1998) were prominent among those which might have been better left unmade, while others were done, fortunately, only as movies for television.

The most negligible remake of all was, indeed, a musical: a 1999 animated redo of *The King and I* to which *Entertainment Weekly* gave a grade of "F" and noted, "In this kingdom, no one whistles a happy tune." In a *vastly* different category was one of the lesser-known films of the iconoclastic cult director

Abel Ferrara, *China Girl* (1987) was, in a way, a warm-up for the Spielberg remake. As per the Ferrara norm, it was stylish, unsettling, and featured a good deal of violence. The rival forces this time were Little Italy and Chinatown, with numerous gangs and a hero named Tony. Essentially, it was an updated, vernacular *Romeo and Juliet*, yet the references to *West Side Story* were both too numerous and too deliberate to overlook, even without Bernstein's music.

In the twenty-first century, with the word "franchise" in common cinematic usage, remakes were folded into the mix of continuations, prequels, and spin-offs. Superhero movies, with their ever-more-sophisticated digital effects and action sequences, could be recycled to deliver the same plotlines with new thrills and maximum amounts of shock and awe. Not dissimilarly, the Walt Disney Company initiated a parade of mega-costly new versions of some of its most successful animated features: *Cinderella, Beauty and the Beast, Dumbo, Aladdin, The Lion King*, and more. The rationale with these and with many twenty-first-century remakes, as a critic observed, "isn't meant to replace or outdo . . . but rather to multiply revenue streams and use a beloved property to show off some new tricks."

This was the movie world that, in 2018, received the news that one of the most successful directors of all time was going to give the world his own take on *West Side Story*. Spielberg himself had been responsible for a popular remake when, in 2005, he directed

War of the Worlds, originally filmed in 1953. But a science-fiction epic is a long distance away from a musical drama, especially one with passionate adherents. Spielberg had only fleeting contact with musical staging, including some raucous dancing in *1941* (1979) and, at the beginning of *Indiana Jones and the Temple of Doom* (1984), an amusing "Anything Goes" sung in Mandarin. Otherwise, his films showed as little interest in musical matters as those directed by Robert Wise in the 1940s and '50s. So how might *West Side Story* fit into this? With success, reputation, and sheer clout beyond the most fanciful dreams of nearly all his peers, Spielberg had long been able to choose exactly the properties he wished to do, be they as serious as *Schindler's List* (1993) or as thrill-intensive as *Jurassic Park* (1993). And, as it turned out, the 1961 original was reported to be one of the few musicals for which Spielberg, movie buff that he was, nursed a good deal of affection.

As seen through an objective lens, there were strong cases to be made both for and against a remake. On the "anti-remake" side, there was both the quality of the first film and the dedication with which it had been made. Far from seeking to crank out another movie-made-from-a-show, the filmmakers sought to preserve the show's integrity by finding a separate-but-equal equivalence. While not making a slavish copy, they stayed unusually close to the source, in some ways strengthening the material. Some of the purely cinematic aspects—the aerial montage, the dynamism of the editing, even the subtle use of special effects—were less movie tricks than genuine enhancements. There is also the matter of the Jerome Robbins choreography which, no matter how imitated, borrowed from, and stolen over the decades, remains sublime. Nor, for that matter, could anyone or anything replicate the fierce commitment and sheer presence of those dancers and actors from whom Robbins demanded so much and to whom he gave a kind of immortality.

Other issues are more equivocal. Obviously, perspectives have changed since *West Side Story* was new, and "the way things were done" in 1960 has since acquired a much different complexion. As with the Broadway original, the film followed the traditions and customs of its time by casting a number of non-Hispanic actors as Puerto Ricans. This, in turn, was compounded by some perceived stereotypes—the Latina spitfire, the macho, crime-prone Latino—and, in the film, makeup and accents that are clearly a product of 1960, not the twenty-first century. ("It was like putting mud on my face," Rita Moreno commented in 2017.) The effects of all this can for some undercut a part of the film's conviction and message. That message, in 1961, had been one of hope: some believed that it might shed fresh light on juvenile delinquency, open dialogue between racially divided groups, and see a path to greater harmony between new immigrants and longtime residents. Six decades later, these problems all persist, and if awareness has been heightened for many, some wounds of division have become even more raw. Of course, there's only so much a film can do, however sincere or false its conventions seem.

There are also some more "movie" factors within the original that may not, to some, seem ideal, such as the vaguely cleaned-up sheen that can betray the site of filming as a Hollywood soundstage. Goodness knows, *West Side Story* is far from the most objectionable in this regard. Still, in spite of the care and expense, there are moments that can seem phony. For some, there is also the question of the songs, both in the occasional incongruity of the dubbed voices and in the aural perspectives that can shift jarringly between speech and singing, between Natalie and Marni. As for the casting: there are aspects of that which will always be in dispute.

The issues connected with culture and ethnicity are especially sensitive and, if anything, some of the response to the Puerto Rican devastation after Hurricane Maria in 2017 made the divisions appear even sharper. Thus it was, in December of 2018, that Steven Spielberg and Tony Kushner traveled to San Juan to have a public discussion about *West Side Story* on the campus of the University of Puerto Rico. With a group of professors, students, and other invited guests in attendance, the conversation stayed off the subject of "representation" for most of its duration. Finally, when one professor brought up what was later termed "the elephant in the room," the discussion began to center around the fact that for many in Puerto Rico, *West Side Story* does not have quite the regard it does on the mainland. In particular, the song "America"

has been viewed as misleading in its implication that most Puerto Ricans emigrate because they despise their homeland. (The fact that Stephen Sondheim changed the lyrics for the film has not prevented the objections from persisting.) Spielberg and Kushner replied to these points by offering assurance that every kind of cultural sensitivity would be applied in making the film, particularly in terms of casting and authentic accents and costuming. If the filmmakers and educators were not always communicating fully with each other, it was a conversation that never would have occurred fifty-eight years earlier, when the first movie was being planned and cast.

While Puerto Rico's general opinion of *West Side Story* appears to be essentially the same now as when the show and movie first opened, it can also be noted that the world viewing Spielberg's *West Side Story* is vastly different from the one that saw the original. Witness, to begin with, the countless changes from then to now in the sheer act of going to the movies. Road-show films are as extinct as the pterodactyl, and filmmakers are under greater pressure than ever before to come up with work whose upfront impact can make an immediate profit. Observe, also, the basic sets of expectations that greeted the first film versus those that inform the remake. In 1961, *West Side Story* was, for all but those who had seen the show, an unknown quantity. Perhaps they knew the music, but there were many millions of people who went to see it and were all but unprepared. What did those audiences feel? The film was so immediate and audacious that its impact was probably like that legendary early movie screening when the spectators in the first rows leaped from their seats to avoid being run down by the train they saw barreling toward the camera. With the poetry and tragedy of the love story, the emotional and physical violence of the conflict, and the constant momentum of the music and dance, this was new, all new.

An audience seeing *West Side Story* in 2020 is carrying far different baggage, both going to the movie theater and then departing it. For one thing, the basic material is far more familiar than it was when the first film opened; everyone, essentially, knows *West Side Story* now. And, among the millions who know and love the original film, apprehension and suspicion about a new version are likely. There's also the fact that a work as consequential and influential as this casts an awfully long shadow. *West Side Story*, the 1961 film, has made an indelible imprint—and how much can be done to shake all that up? Or, even less likely, eclipse it? In an interview he gave before his trip to Puerto Rico, Tony Kushner stressed that his script for the new film will follow the original show far more than the movie—although, in actuality, those two entities had not been very far apart. Careful to not criticize the original film, which he termed a "masterpiece," Kushner added that the new version is intended not to replace its predecessor but "to be a new interpretation. . . . There are many different versions possible of a great work of art like *West Side Story*, and we are doing our own version."

Kushner's statements are certainly accurate, and they make an important point. Regardless of merit or quality, a film can be remade, but it cannot be replaced. If comparisons are unavoidable, the basic 1961 film does not change. Unlike stage productions, which are essentially ephemeral, a film is, in a particular way, everlasting. While perceptions and opinions may shift and alter, the basic work will remain. In this case, the work has always been, and will always be, of very high quality indeed. This was true on Broadway in 1957, remained so on film in 1961, and forever after.

As to the Spielberg film, one of the members of the original cast offered an elegant bit of torch-passing. Carole D'Andrea, who created the role of Velma on Broadway and reprised it in the film, has said, "It is so wonderful they are giving a new generation a chance to make and experience this beautiful classic."

One further certainty remains. *West Side Story*, as codirected by Robert Wise and Jerome Robbins, will continue to thrill, delight, and even sometimes provoke its audiences. Through all that work and conflict back in 1960 and 1961—the injuries, delays, headaches, and firings—somehow, it happened. It triumphed when it was new, and it still does. On screens big and small, Maria and Tony and the Jets and the Sharks will remain vivid, immediate, and unforgettable. They will not change. Nor will they be replaced.

OPPOSITE: The official casting call announcement, as posted on Twitter

CASTING CALL

20TH CENTURY FOX
DIRECTED BY **STEVEN SPIELBERG**
ADAPTED BY **TONY KUSHNER**

SEARCHING FOR TONY, MARIA, ANITA & BERNARDO
- **TONY** is CAUCASIAN • **MARIA** & **ANITA** are LATINA • **BERNARDO** is LATINO
- SHOULD BE BETWEEN 15 - 25 YEARS OLD
- MUST BE ABLE TO SING
- STRONG DANCE BACKGROUND REQUIRED

WEST SIDE STORY

To submit,
please email a photo & video of yourself singing to
westsidestorycastingsearch@gmail.com

SOMEWHERE

ABOVE: Bernardo and Riff: Chakiris and Tamblyn, with Larry Roquemore at rear

PAGE 188: The last scene

PERCEPTIONS, PROCEDURES, tastes, customs, movies, politics, people. They *all* change. It is impossible to confront *West Side Story* as people did in 1961, when they excitedly clipped the order blank from their newspapers to send away for tickets, then waited weeks and months to see if it could live up to the reports, the reviews, the word of mouth. For nearly all of them, it did so, and they eagerly passed the word along and even went back to see it again. All of that is in the past, along with so much else that seemed to matter when *West Side Story* was first playing in theaters. So much about it must be seen differently now—and yet nothing keeps it from asserting its importance, worth, and permanence.

Unquestionably, the show that gave birth to the film is a work of lasting greatness,

extraordinary in both its quality and its relevance. Some have said that it far outdoes the movie in that regard, but is that really the case? Theater often views cinema with disdain, so look again at the film. Are there moments of greatness that are any less worthy than on the stage? Are the finest parts of the movie anything less than indelible? Some may say "yes," while for many others the answers to these questions are all "no." If it was the product of a medium that can be crass and irrelevant, it was blessed to be the creation of people whose skills, intentions, aspirations, and sincerity were vastly above the norm. Between the mastery of Jerome Robbins, the unwavering expertise and craft of Robert Wise, and the dedication of its cast, musicians, artists, staff, and technicians, its possibilities were realized to an unprecedented degree. For all its long and complicated creative process, there was a final outcome that justified everything.

Obviously, we cannot see *West Side Story* through those same "I've heard about it, now stun me!" eyes people had in 1961. Nevertheless, there are moments that are so arresting, so exceptional or inimitable, that they give a clue to the initial excitement people felt when they saw it. Everyone has notions regarding the film's special and unique moments, those things not found in any other movie, nor in any other production of *West Side Story*. They belong only here, and everyone who cares about this film has her or his own list. What follows, then, is a sampling.

- ✶ The three-note whistle. It's the first sound heard in the film, before the overture. Then, even more eerily, it's heard again with that bracing aerial shot of the George Washington Bridge. Even for those who don't know *West Side Story*, it seems to portend that this may not end happily.

- ✶ The uneasy thrill of the overhead zoom down to the Jets in the playground, which cuts to the arresting first view of Russ Tamblyn in profile, accompanied by that finger snap.

- ✶ George Chakiris, flanked by Jay Norman and Eddie Verso, dancing in the Prologue, as photographed from a low angle that frames the trio against a row of tenements. The shot of them with left legs extended high became iconic, and no wonder.

- ✶ The recurring motif of doors. If the fire escapes offer hope, perhaps those endless lines of doors in the Prologue (and elsewhere, including the final credits) signify something more ominous. No way out, perhaps. In a far different vein are the multicolored glass panes in the doors to Maria's bedroom. Do they serve as the portal to the bright world shared only by Tony and Maria? Whatever they are, they're unforgettable.

- ✶ Carole D'Andrea as Velma, with her odd and mesmerizing combination of the ethereal and the tough, the detached and the engaged, as seen first in the gym dance and then, later, during "Cool."

- ✶ The hypnotic moment, both theatrical and cinematic, when the other dancers, and then the walls, melt away as Maria and Tony see each other for the first time.

- ✶ Yvonne Othon, as Consuelo, during the verse before "America." Reacting to Rita Moreno's "I love the isle of Manhattan," she exclaims an ad-libbed "I know you do!" in flawless "Nuyorican."

- ✶ The banter and rapport, snappy, affectionate, and knowing, between George Chakiris and Rita Moreno in "America."

- ✶ The dreamy close-up of Natalie Wood in "Tonight," when Jim Bryant sings "Today, all day I had the feeling."

- ✶ The vaudeville-style banter of "Gee, Officer Krupke." For some, it belongs in another, more traditional show, but just listen to those abrasive, sardonic lyrics.

- ✶ The offhand delight, during "I Feel Pretty," of Yvonne Othon chewing gum and singing backup at the same time.

- ✶ The extreme and even shocking cut, visual and aural, from the beatific "One Hand, One Heart" to the blaring and blazing start of the "Tonight Quintet."

- ✶ The editing of the "Tonight Quintet," which becomes faster, more percussive and virtuosic, as the sequence progresses. The number has been rethought so effectively that most later productions have found it necessary to draw from it.

- The expression on Russ Tamblyn's face when Riff realizes that the Rumble has gotten "real," quickly followed by that famous first flash of the switchblade.

- The "Cool it, A-Rab" moment in the garage, with David Winters giving an unflinching demonstration of gang-member instability. The wonder of "Cool," in fact, is that the whole of it is pretty much up to that level.

- The fury, pain, and conviction that inform Rita Moreno's "Don't you touch me!" The entire scene has been so painful to watch that it needed this strong passage to move it to the devastating conclusion of "He shot her!"

- Natalie Wood in the final scene, snarling the word "trigger" and crying out "I can kill, too," with blazing eyes. Then, the dignity of her exit, a solitary figure in red and black.

- The conclusion of the final credits, with the camera tilting upward to the first word of the sign "END OF STREET." Robert Wise had done something similar in his previous film, *Odds Against Tomorrow*. There, the sign read, "STOP DEAD END." This one seems even more final.

The very last strains of "Somewhere," which end the film as they did the show, have a haunting and haunted quality that is deeply felt but not at all conclusive. As a corpse is carried out, followed by a "widow" and mourners, the music lingers without finding resolution, refusing to bring a tidy end to what has come before. Leonard Bernstein's daughter Jamie, reflecting on that passage, remarked on the sad and inevitable truths carried by these bars of music. "So that's how *West Side Story* ends," she says. "Or is the world getting better? Is there hope for us to find a better place to all live together in harmony? Hmmmmm . . . not sure."

No, the show's creators couldn't be sure about there being hope. Nor could the filmmakers. Both on stage and in extra-wide Panavision 70, *West Side Story* wants to reach toward hope, but reality keeps pulling it back. That back-and-forth struggle has been expressed through some of the most resourceful songs ever written for a musical, some of most innovative and character-driven choreography of all time, and, on film, a dedication to the craft that goes far beyond the aspirations of most musicals. Up to and including those final notes, the artists and filmmakers have been honest—in a *musical*, yet—to a degree that could not be approached by most people who make movies. Indeed, one of the everlasting beauties of *West Side Story* is that it doesn't suddenly turn false at the end, promising a solution where none can be found. It's tragic and heart-rending yet also clear-eyed, and by doing this it stays true to itself and respectful of its audience. This is the kind of achievement that is possible when people believe in what they're doing and in the film they're making. With this degree of integrity, and with all the care, artistry, and feeling available to them, they made a monument that will continue to endure. For six decades and counting, this movie has not grown dim or become less captivating. Nor has it passed away. "Even death won't part us now," Tony and Maria sing. They're completely right.

OPPOSITE: "Cool it, A-Rab": David Winters in "Cool"

FILM CREDITS

DESPITE THE LENGTHY LIST OF CAST AND CREW NAMES AT THE END OF *WEST SIDE STORY*, a number of cast and crew members were not given credit on the screen. Additionally, a number of cast members would later, for professional or personal reasons, be known by different names. In this list, the credited cast and crew members are followed by those who were not listed on-screen. The actors' alternate or subsequent names are given in parentheses.

PRODUCTION CREDITS

- Presented by Mirisch Pictures Inc., in association with Seven Arts Productions Inc.
- A Robert Wise (Beta) Production
- Released Through United Artists

CAST (IN CREDITED ORDER)

- Maria: Natalie Wood
- Tony: Richard Beymer
- Riff: Russ Tamblyn
- Anita: Rita Moreno
- Bernardo: George Chakiris
- Schrank: Simon Oakland
- Doc: Ned Glass
- Krupke: William Bramley
- Ice: Tucker Smith
- Action: Tony Mordente
- A-Rab: David Winters

OPPOSITE: Tony and Maria

- Baby John: Eliot Feld
- Snowboy: Bert Michaels
- Tiger: David Bean
- Joyboy: Robert Banas
- Big Deal: Scooter (Anthony) Teague
- Mouthpiece: Harvey Hohnecker (Evans)
- Gee-Tar: Tommy Abbott
- Anybodys: Susan Oakes
- Graziella: Gina Trikonis
- Velma: Carole D'Andrea
- Chino: Jose De Vega
- Pepe: Jay Norman
- Indio: Gus Trikonis
- Juano: Eddie Verso
- Loco: Jaime Rogers
- Rocco: Larry Roquemore
- Luis: Robert Thompson
- Toro: Nick Covacevich (Navarro)
- Del Campov: Rudy Del Campo

- Chile: Andre Tayir

- Consuelo: Yvonne Othon (Wilder)

- Rosalia: Suzie Kaye

- Francisca: Joanne Miya (Nobuko Miyamoto)

ADDITIONAL CAST (IN ALPHABETICAL ORDER)

- Boy on bicycle: Martin Abrahams

- Glad Hand: John Astin

- Debby, Snowboy's Girlfriend: Francesca Bellini

- Boy on basketball court: Christopher (Kit) Culkin

- Clarice, Big Deal's Girlfriend: Rita Hyde (D'Amico)

- Teresita, Juano's Girlfriend: Maria Jimenez (Henley)

- Hotsie, Tiger's Girlfriend: Elaine Joyce

- Little Girl (extra): Priscilla Lopez

- Margarita, Rocco's Girlfriend: Olivia Perez

- Police Officer No. 3: Lou Ruggiero

- Madam Lucia: Penny Santon

- Estella, Loco's Girlfriend: Luci Stone

- Minnie, Baby John's Girlfriend: Pat Tribble

- Dancer: Gary Troy

- Dancer: Roxanne Tunis

CREDITS (IN ON-SCREEN ORDER)

- Directors: Robert Wise and Jerome Robbins

- Screenplay: Ernest Lehman

- Music: Leonard Bernstein

- Lyrics: Stephen Sondheim

- Associate producer: Saul Chaplin

- Choreography: Jerome Robbins

- Musical conductor: Johnny Green

- Production design: Boris Leven

- Director of photography: Daniel L. Fapp

- Costume design: Irene Sharaff

- Assistant director: Robert E. Relyea

- Dance assistants: Tommy Abbott, Margaret Banks, Howard Jeffrey, Tony Mordente

- Film editor: Thomas Stanford

- Music editor: Richard Carruth

- Photographic effects: Linwood Dunn, Film Effects of Hollywood

- Orchestrations: Sid Ramin, Irwin Kostal

- Sound: Murray Spivack, Fred Lau, Vinton Vernon

- Musical assistant: Betty Walberg

- Vocal coach: Bobby Tucker

- Musical supervision: Saul Chaplin, Johnny Green, Sid Ramin, Irwin Kostal

- Production manager: Allen K. Wood

- Titles and visual consultation: Saul Bass

- Production artist: M(aurice) Zuberano

- Set decorator: Victor Gangelin

- Properties: Sam Gordon

- Sound editor: Gilbert D. Marchant

- Assistant editor: Marshall M. Borden

- Script supervisor: Stanley K. Scheuer

- Second assistant director: Jerome M. Siegel

- Makeup: Emile La Vigne

- Hairdresser: Alice Monte

- Wardrobe: Bert Henrikson

- Casting: Stalmaster-Lister Co.

- Based upon the stage play produced by Robert E. Griffith and Harold S. Prince, by arrangement with Roger L. Stevens; book by Arthur Laurents; music by Leonard Bernstein; lyrics by Stephen Sondheim; play conceived, directed, and choreographed by Jerome Robbins

- Filmed in Technicolor and Panavision 70

ADDITIONAL CREDITS

- Executive producer: Walter Mirisch

- Production executive: Harold Mirisch

- Production executive: Marvin Mirisch

- Production manager: Hubert Fröhlich

- Scenic artist: Shelley Bartolini

- Production illustrator: Leon Harris

- Construction coordinator: William Maldonado

- Sound mixer: Richard Gramaglia

- Sound recording supervisor: Fred Hynes

- Sound supervisor: Gordon Sawyer

- Stunts: Eli Bo, Jack Blackfeather

- Camera operator, title sequence: John Finger

- Still photographer: Ernst Haas

- Electrician: Jerome H. Klein

- Dolly grip, title sequence: Louis Kulsey

- Grip: Tom May

- Still photographer: Phil Stern

- Script supervisor: John Flynn

- Playback music operator: Walter A. Gest

- Press representative: Howard Newman

- Musicians (selected): Pete Candoli (trumpet), Gene Cipriano (woodwinds), Jack Dumont (saxophone), Al Hendrickson (guitar), Shelly Manne (drums), Red Mitchell (acoustic double bass), Dave Pell (saxophone), Uan Rasey (trumpet), Howard Roberts (guitar), Ray Turner, Ray Sherman (piano), Lloyd Ulyate (trombone), Al Viola (guitar), Marni Nixon (singing voice, Maria), Jimmy Bryant (singing voice, Tony), Betty Wand (singing voice, Anita—partial), Tucker Smith (singing voice, Riff—partial)

CITATIONS

USC refers to the University of Southern California in Los Angeles,
Cinematic Arts Library, Special Collections.

CHAPTER 1

11 "'Romeo To Receive": *New York Times*, January 27, 1949.

11 You'll never write it": Nora Kaye, quoted in Arthur Laurents, "The Birth of an Idea," *New York Herald-Tribune*, August 4, 1957.

17 "I just loved him": Chita Rivera, quoted in Deborah Jowitt, *Jerome Robbins: His Life, His Theater, His Dance* (New York: Simon & Schuster, 2004), p. 276.

17-18 Robbins's fall: One of the more recent of the many accounts of this event, which gives cast member/writer/lyricist/director Martin Charnin as the source, is Barbara Hoffman, "Actors Recall living in Fear of Jerome Robbins—Yet Dying to Work with Him," *New York Post*, July 26, 2018.

19 "Oh God" Carol Lawrence, *Carol Lawrence: The Backstage Story* (New York: McGraw Hill, 1990), p. 2.

20-21 Reviews of *West Side Story*: All ran in the named publications on September 27, 1957. "Juke-box Manhattan opera": comment by John Chapman in *The New York Daily News*. The *New Yorker* review ran in the issue of October 5, 1957.

24 Bernstein and Sondheim option: Agreement between Bernstein, Sondheim, and Seven Arts Productions, November 5, 1958. Courtesy of confidential source.

Contractual considerations: Walter Mirisch to author via Larry Mirisch email to author, July 27, 2019.

CHAPTER 2

27 "Let us take": Boris Leven, undated memo [ca. 1959] to Robert Wise. Boris Leven Collection, USC, Box 9 file 20.

31 "Billy Wilder told us": Walter Mirisch, *I Thought We Were Making Movies, Not History* (Madison: The University of Wisconsin Press, 2008), p. 100.

34 "The only person": Saul Chaplin, interviewed in *Max Wilk, They're Playing Our Song* (New York: Zoetrope, 1986), p. 226.

37 "Anyone on the street": Ernest Lehman, notes taken during New York research trip, Ernest Lehman Collection, USC, Box 27 folder 1.

37 "Unacceptably sex-suggestive": Geoffrey M. Shurlock, letter to Walter M. Mirisch, June 28, 1960, *West Side Story* MPAA

[Motion Picture Association of America] file, Margaret Herrick Library, Academy of Motion Picture Arts & Sciences.

38-39 Johnny Green anecdotes: Saul Chaplin, *The Golden Age of Hollywood Musicals and Me* (University of Oklahoma Press, 1994), pp 176 ff.

39 "We decided": Sid Ramin, quoted in Anita Gates, "Sid Ramin, 100, Who Put Music to Broadway Hits, Woolite and Ultra Brite, Too," *The New York Times*, July 6, 2019.

CHAPTER 3

42 "Casting the film": Saul Chaplin, *The Golden Age*, p. 179.

44 Elizabeth Taylor: George Chakiris, *CBS Sunday Morning* interview, February 24, 2019.

46 "A very different time": Rita Moreno, interviewed for *In the Thick* podcast #44, "The Many Accents of Rita Moreno," National Public Radio, January 10, 2017.

48 Wise notes: Unless stated otherwise, all the quotes about casting are from Robert Wise's casting notes, in the Robert Wise Collection at USC, Box 34, file 2.

49 Moreno wrote: *Rita Moreno: A Memoir* (New York: Celebra, 2013), p. 161.

50 "A United Artists executive": Mirisch, *I Thought*, p. 124.

53 "Good voice": Leonard Bernstein datebook, May 16, 1957, Leonard Bernstein Collection, the Library of Congress.

53 "He might have been chosen": Chaplin, *The Golden Age*, p. 181.

57 "Hundreds of dudes": Nick Covacevich, *Our Story: Jets & Sharks Then and Now* (Denver: Outskirts Press, Inc., 2011), p. 214.

58-59 Taffy Paul" Carole D'Andrea, email to author, August 4, 2019; also, Kate Whitehead, "My life: Stefanie Powers," *Post Magazine*, December 7, 2013.

62 Russ Tamblyn and MGM: Tamblyn, interviewed in Patrick McDonald, "Stars of 'West Side Story' for 50th Anniversary," www.hollywoodchicago.com, November 24, 2011.

62 "Annamariaspaghetti" and ff Jerome Robbins:, undated letter (ca. April 1960) to Robert Wise, Wise Collection, USC box 34, folder 16.

63 "Ludicrous": Chaplin, *The Golden Age*, p. 180.

62 "A fawn in the forest": Robert Relyea, with Craig Relyea, *Not So Quiet On the Set* (New York: iUniverse, 2008), p. 151.

63 "It was a test" Robert Wise, interview in *West Side Stories*, unreleased documentary, 1995.

63 Diane Baker: Diane Baker, email interview with author, August 16, 2019.

CHAPTER 4

67 "Robbins wanted perfection": Robert Banas, *Our Story*, 108.

69 "When you think": "Small Rumble," *The New Yorker*, April 2, 1960.

69ff Lincoln Square and locations: The website popspotsnyc.com contains a detailed rundown of the shooting sites used for *West Side Story*, matching frames from the film with actual photos of the neighborhood.

71 Ursaner, Eagle Demolition: Allen K. Wood, memo to Bob Relyea, July 13, 1960, Wise Collection, USC, Box 34, folder 13.

71 "Five or ten thousand": Robert Wise, quoted in Greg Lawrence, *Dance with Demons: The Life of Jerome Robbins* (New York: Berkley, 2001), p. 289.

74 "A kind of abstract": Wise, interview in *West Side Stories.*

74 "I held his belt": Robert Relyea, interview in *West Side Stories.*

74ff More cast members and locations: Relyea, memo to Wood, June 6, 1960; New York Location List, (Undated, ca. July 6, 1960), Wise Collection, USC Box 34, folder 13.

76 "Once it's on film": Russ Tamblyn, quoted in Lawrence, *Dance With Demons*, p. 290.

77 "Artistic snobs": David Winters, *Tough Guys Do Dance* (Pensacola: Indigo Rivers Publishing, 2018), p. 88.

77 "We were used": Harvey Evans, interviewed on *Theater Talk*, CUNY-TV, November 12, 2012.

80 Winters, Mordente, Othon, D'Andrea quotes interviews in *West Side Stories*

80 "His eyes": Gina Trikonis, *Our Stories*, p. 152.

80 "If you worked hard": David Bean, *Theater Talk* interview, CUNY-TV, November 12, 2012.

80 "A concentration camp" and ff Chaplin: *The Golden Age*, p. 187.

81 Tamblyn & Chakiris: McDonald, "Stars of '*West Side Story*'"

81 "We all did": Bert Michaels, *Our Stories*, p. 38.

81 "I want the movements": Jerome Robbins, interview in Bill Becker, "Hollywood Steps," *The New York Times* July 3, 1960.

82 "As any riot": Relyea, interviewed in *West Side Stories.*

82 "Twenty wild animals": Relyea, interviewed in *West Side Stories.*

83 "The casualty list": Relyea, *Not So Quiet*, p. 156.

87 "Jerry would say": Margaret Banks, quoted in Lawrence, *Dance With Demons*, p. 289.

87 "The hardest time": Rita Moreno, interviewed in *West Side Stories.*

CHAPTER 5

90 "How did they": Tony Mordente, *Our Story*, p. 30.

93 "Geez Jerry": Russ Tamblyn, quoted in "Movers and Shakers of Movie Musicals," *People*, April 8, 2002.

93 "The New York film": Harold J. Mirisch, memo to Robert Wise and Jerome Robbins, September 12, 1960, Wise Collection, USC, box 34 folder 13.

93 "These items": Harold J. Mirisch, memo to Wise and Robbins, September 15, 1960. Wise Collection, USC box 34 folder 3.

93 "She wasn't Chita": Carole d'Andrea, quoted in Lawrence, *Dance With Demons*, p. 287.

94 "The wall doesn't work": Yvonne Othon [Wilder], interviewed in *West Side Stories*

94 "You know you think": Rita Moreno, interviewed in *West Side Stories*.

94 Garage set: Herb A Lightman, "The Photography of 'West Side Story'" *American Cinematographer*, December 1961.

95 "We were supposed": Gina Trikonis, *Our Story*, pp. 147-48.

96 "I don't ever believe": Relyea, interviewed in *West Side Stories*.

98 "This is Natalie": Bert Michaels, *Our Story*, pp. 39-40.

98 "Awful": Rita Moreno, quoted in Suzanne Finstad, *Natasha: The Biography of Natalie Wood* (New York: Harmony Books, 2001), p. 231. Wood had previously attempted a Mexican accent in the 1956 film *The Burning Hills*, without great success.

98 Nightclub act: Finstad, *Natasha*, pp. 186-87.

98 "It looked as if": Robert Wise, letter to Paul F. Johnson, September 18, 1961. Wise Collection, USC box 34 folder 4, "Congratulatory Letters."

99 "The entire music department": Marni Nixon, *I Could Have Sung All Night*, with Stephen Cole (New York: Billboard Books, 2006), p. 134.

101 "In a way": Mart Crowley, quoted in Lawrence, *Dance with Demons*, p. 287.

101 "Very demanding": Robert Wise, quoted in Lawrence, *Dance with Demons*, p. 288.

101 "Jerry just didn't pay": Mart Crowley, quoted in Lawrence, *Dance with Demons*, p. 292.

101 By October 10: Shooting script for *West Side Story*, annotated by Script Supervisor Stanley K. Scheuer. Starting with October 10, Scheuer would list each day's total of footage and script pages, plus the cumulative totals thus far. Stanley Scheuer Collection, USC, file G no. 11.

103 "Want you to know": Harold J. Mirisch, memo to Robert Wise, Jerome Robbins, and Al Wood, October 5, 1960, Wise Collection, USC, box 34 folder 13.

103 "Under no circumstances": Harold J. Mirisch, memo to Robert Wise, Jerome Robbins, and Al Wood, October 11, 1960, Wise Collection, USC, box 34 folder 13.

103 "Print it anyway": Margaret Banks, quoted in Jowitt, *Jerome Robbins*, p. 287.

103-4 "I want to caution you": Harold J. Mirisch, memo to Wise and Robbins, September 12, 1960, Wise Collection, USC, box 34 folder 13.

104 "Don't lose": Tony Mordente, *Our Story*, p. 27.

104 $6.75 million: Mirisch, *I Thought*, p. 127. Verified by Mr. Mirisch in Larry Mirisch email to author, July 27, 2019.

105 "Coup . . . assassination": Relyea, *Not So Quiet*, p. 154.

105 "We concentrated": Mirisch, *I Thought*, p. 126.

106 "A terrible scene": and ff Walter Mirisch, *I Thought*, p. 126.

106 "None of you": Gina Trikonis, *Our Story*, p. 154.

106-7 "Was just sitting": Mart Crowley, quoted in Lawrence, *Dance with Demons*, p. 292.

107 "[*Ambersons*] probably was": Robert Wise, quoted in Barbara Leaming, *Orson Welles* (New York: Viking, 1985), p. 293.

107 "The ballet should": Robert Wise, memo to Bob Relyea, June 13, 1960, Boris Leven Collection, USC, box 14 folder 48.

124 "Just the nature": Robert Wise, quoted in Lawrence, *Dance With Demons*, p. 291.

124 "I felt sorry": Tony Mordente, quoted in Lawrence, *Dance With Demons*, p. 292.

124 "Far and away": Saul Chaplin, *The Golden Age*, p. 181.

124 "It's a thankless role": Richard Beymer, interviewed in Julie Wheelock, "'Twin Peaks' Stars Tamblyn, Beymer Share Twin Experience", *Los Angeles Times*, April 6, 1990.

128 "You didn't have to": Russ Tamblyn, interviewed in Wheelock, "'Twin Peaks' Stars."

128 January 4: Robert (Bob) Relyea, memo to Allen (Al) Wood, November 3, 1960. Wise Collection, USC, box 34, folder 14.

128 "I *was* Anita": Rita Moreno, interviewed in *West Side Stories.*

129 February 14: *West Side Story* Work Script, Scheuer Collection, USC, File G No. 11.

129 Chaplin . . . said later: Saul Chaplin, interviewed in *West Side Stories.* The specific quote is, "I knew from the very beginning that we had to dub Natalie Wood."

129 Beymer once mentioned: Marni Nixon, *I Could Have Sung*, p. 135.

131 "The main problem": Jerome Robbins, Notes on rough cut of film, April 12, 1961 Wise Collection, USC, box 34 folder 16.

134 "I feel I am": Robert Wise, memo to Raymond Kurtzman, May 24, 1961, Wise Collection, USC, box 34 folder 16.

136 "Nothing is really impossible": Linwood G. Dunn, draft of *West Side Story* proposal to the Mirisch Company, April 16, 1960 Linwood G. Dunn papers (f.475), Margaret Herrick Library, Academy of Motion Picture Arts and Sciences.

INTERMISSION

143 $7,500: Leonard Bernstein contract (February 21, 1961) with Beta Productions (the corporation formed jointly by Mirisch Pictures and Robert Wise). Courtesy of confidential source.

144 "America": Stephen Sondheim contract (June 15, 1960) with Beta Productions/ Mirisch/Seven Arts specifies "Completely new lyrics for the song entitled 'America.'" Courtesy of confidential source.

144 Doc's line: Ernest Lehman, annotations on *West Side Story* script drafts, Lehman Collection, USC, box 34 folder 1.

CHAPTER 6

149 Joseph Caroff: See http://sergottart. com/artists/joseph-caroff/biography/.

151 "Life is great": Rita Moreno interview with Irene Thirer, "Rita Moreno Tells 'West Side Story,'" *New York Post*, August 28, 1961.

151: *Variety* review: Whitney Williams, September 27, 1961.

151-2 *Hollywood Reporter* review: James Powers, "'West Side Story' Hailed as B.O. Smash, Great Film Work" September 22, 1961.

152 Arthur Knight review: *Saturday Review*, October 14, 1961.

152 Stanley Kauffmann review: *The New Republic*, October 23, 1961; reprinted (with a postscipt) in Stanley Kauffmann, *A World on Film* (New York: Dell, 1966), pp. 134-37.

153 *New Yorker* review: Brendan Gill, October 21, 1961.

153 *Newsweek* review: October 23, 1961.

153 *Time* review: October 20, 1961.

153 Pauline Kael review: Kael, *I Lost It at the Movies* (New York: Little Brown, 1965), pp. 141-48.

154 *National Geographic* photo: October 1962.

156 "A weird beauty or personality": Scott's comments on the awards were widely reported, as by Erskine Johnson in his syndicated "Hollywood Today!" column, March 1962.

157 "I went to the Academy Awards": Mart Crowley, interviewed in Lawrence, *Dance With Demons*, p. 292.

158 "It wasn't easy": Relyea, *Not So Quiet*, p. 157.

158 "But at least": Hedda Hopper, quoted in (among other sources) Mason Wiley and Damien Bona, *Inside Oscar: The Unofficial History of the Academy Awards* (New York: Ballantine, 1987), p. 340.

158 "Some of it gets": Jerome Robbins, letter to Richard Buckle, October 16, 1961, quoted in Jowitt, *Jerome Robbins*, p. 292.

158 "They're bland": Robbins, letter to Buckle, May 30, 1961, quoted in Jowitt, *Jerome Robbins*, p. 292.

159 "Don't think I'm smart": Natalie Wood, interview by Murray Kempton, "Natalie Wood: Is *This* the Girl Next Door?" *Show*, March 1962.

159 "When records became": Marni Nixon, *I Could Have Sung*, p. 137.

159 Betty Wand: see Jack Gottlieb, "Fact

Sheet," westsidestory.com/archives-1.

160 "Unlike other classics": *West Side Story* trailer, Youtube.com Although listed in some places as the original 1961 trailer, this is for the 1968 reissue.

160-62 share and violence: John J. O'Connor, "Was 'West Side Story' Bad for East Harlem?" *The New York Times*, April 2, 1972.

CHAPTER 7

163 "So how do you follow": Nobuko Miyamoto (Joanne Miya), *Our Stories*, p. 232.

164 "[I wish] someone": Russ Tamblyn, interviewed in *West Side Stories*.

166 "His greatest role": *Satan's Sadists* trailer, YouTube.

166 "In entertainment": Russtamblyn.com.

166-7 "The kind of movie": Glenn Erickson, *CineSavant* (formerly *DVD Savant*) review, June 12, 2007, dvdtalk.com.

169 "In my mind": Richard Beymer, interviewed in Wheelock, "'Twin Peaks' Stars."

170 "This time the services": Mirisch, *I Thought*, p. 305.

171 "He wasn't inclined": David Ehrenstein, "Still pretty and witty and gay," *The Advocate*, April 29, 2003.

171 "Don't forget to smell": Robert Banas, *Our Stories*, p 132.

172 "Uses art": GreatLeap.org.

172 "Lamentable": Chaplin, *The Golden Age*, p. 251.

173 "The thing is": Jerome Robbins, interviewed in Emily Coleman, "From Tutus to T-Shirts," *New York Times Magazine*, October 8, 1961.

174 "Wise has worn": Hal Hinson, the *Washington Post*, March 18, 1989.

177 "Really crappy": Rita Moreno, interviewed on *Live With Kelly and Ryan*, ABC-TV, February 22, 2019.

179 "The brightest star": Margaret Lyons, review of *One Day at a Time*, *New York Times*, January 25, 2018.

CHAPTER 8

180 "You want to talk": Rita Moreno, interviewed in Bryan Brunati, "Rita Moreno, 87, Says 'There's No Plastic Here' When It comes to Her Looks," Closerweekly.com, March 16, 2019.

183 "In this kingdom": Lisa Schwarzbaum, review of *The King and I*, *Entertainment Weekly*, March 26, 1999.

183 "Isn't meant to replace": A. O. Scott, review of *The Lion King*, *The New York Times*, July 11, 2019.

184 "It was like putting mud": Rita Moreno, interview on "In The Thick" podcast, NPR, January 10, 2017.

185 "The elephant in the room": Isel Rodriguez, quoted in Seth Abramovitch, "Steven Spielberg Met With Puerto Ricans about 'West Side Story' Concerns," *The Hollywood Reporter*, January 15, 2019.

186 "Masterpiece" and ff: Tony Kushner, quoted in Paul Chi, "Steven Spielberg's West Side Story Will Go Back to Basics," *Vanity Fair*, online version, October 23, 2018.

186 "It is so wonderful": Carole D'Andrea, email to author, August 4, 2019.

EPILOGUE

192 "So that's how": Jamie Bernstein, speaking in *West Side Stories: The Making of a Classic* BBC documentary, 2016.

SELECTED BIBLIOGRAPHY

BOOKS

Acevedo-Muñoz, Ernesto R. *West Side Story as Cinema: The Making and Impact of an American Masterpiece*. Lawrence, KS: University Press of Kansas, 2013.

Banas, Robert, ed. *Our Story: Jets & Sharks Then and Now*. Denver: Outskirts Press, 2011.

Bernstein, Jamie. *Famous Father Girl: A Memoir of Growing Up Bernstein*. New York: HarperCollins, 2018.

Berson, Misha. *Something's Coming, Something Good:* West Side Story *and the American Imagination*. Milwaukee: Applause Theatre & Cinema Books, 2011.

Beymer, Richard. *Impostor: or Whatever Happened to Richard Beymer?* (An unauthorized autobiography). Self-published, 2007.

Bowman, Manoah, and Natasha Gregson Wagner. *Natalie Wood: Reflections on a Legendary Life*. Philadelphia: Running Press, 2016.

Burton, Humphrey. *Leonard Bernstein*. New York: Doubleday, 1994.

Chaplin, Saul. *The Golden Age of Movie Musicals and Me*. Norman, OK: University of Oklahoma Press, 1994.

Finstad, Suzanne. *Natasha: The Biography of Natalie Wood*. New York: Harmony Books, 2001.

Foulkes, Julia L. *A Place for Us:* West Side Story *and New York*. Chicago: The University of Chicago Press, 2016.

Garebian, Keith. *The Making of* West Side Story. Toronto: ECW Press, 1995.

Gehring, Wes D. *Robert Wise: Shadowlands*. Indianapolis: Indiana Historical Society Press, 2012.

Jordan, Joe. *Robert Wise: The Motion Pictures*. Joseph R. Jordan, 2017.

Jowitt, Deborah. *Jerome Robbins: His Life, His Theater, His Dance*. New York: Simon & Schuster, 2004.

Kael, Pauline. *I Lost It at the Movies: Film Writings 1954–1965*. Boston: Little, Brown, 1965.

Kauffmann, Stanley. *A World on Film: Criticism and Comment*. New York: Harper & Row, 1966.

Laurents, Arthur. *Mainly on Directing: Gypsy, West Side Story, and Other Musicals*. New York: Alfred A. Knopf, 2009.

———. *Original Story By: A Memoir of Broadway and Hollywood*. New York: Applause Theatre Books, 2000.

Laurents, Arthur, and Leonard Bernstein, Stephen Sondheim, and Jerome Robbins. *West Side Story: A Musical*. (Based on a conception of Jerome Robbins) New York, Random House, 1957.

Lawrence, Carol. *Carol Lawrence: The Backstage Story*. New York: McGraw-Hill, 1990.

Lawrence, Greg. *Dance with Demons: The Life of Jerome Robbins*. New York: Berkley Books, 2001.

Leaming, Barbara. *Orson Welles*. New York: Viking, 1985.

Mirisch, Walter. *I Thought We Were Making Movies, Not History*. Madison, WI: The University of Wisconsin Press, 2008.

Monush, Barry. *Music on Film: West Side Story*. Milwaukee: Limelight Editions, 2010.

Mordden, Ethan. *Anything Goes: A History of American Musical Theatre*. New York: Oxford University Press, 2013.

Mordden, Ethan. *Coming Up Roses: The Broadway Musical in the 1950s*. New York: Oxford University Press, 2000.

Moreno, Rita. *Rita Moreno: A Memoir*. New York: Celebra, 2013.

Nixon, Marni, and Stephen Cole. *I Could Have Sung All Night: My Story*. New York: Billboard Books, 2006.

Peyser, Joan. *Bernstein: A Biography*. New York: Beech Tree Books, 1987.

Relyea, Robert E., and Craig Relyea. *Not So Quiet on the Set: My Life in Movies During Hollywood's Macho Era*. New York: iUniverse, Inc., 2008.

Shulman, Irving. West Side Story: *A Novelization*. New York: Pocket Books, 1961.

Secrest, Meryle. *Leonard Bernstein: A Life*. New York: Alfred A. Knopf, 1994.

Sharaff, Irene. *Broadway & Hollywood: Costumes Designed by Irene Sharaff*. New York: Van Nostrand Reinhold, 1976.

Simeone, Nigel, ed. *The Leonard Bernstein Letters*. New Haven, CT: Yale University Press, 2018.

Simeone, Nigel. *Leonard Bernstein:* West Side Story. London: Routledge, 2009.

Vaill, Amanda. *Somewhere: The Life of Jerome Robbins*. New York: Broadway Books, 2006.

Wells, Elizabeth A. West Side Story*: Cultural Perspectives on an American Musical*. Lanham, MD: Scarecrow Press, 2011.

West Side Story. Souvenir program for the film. New York: Program Publishing Company, 1961.

Wiley, Mason, and Damien Bona. *Inside Oscar: The Unofficial History of the Academy Awards*. Updated Edition. New York: Ballantine Books, 1987.

Wilk, Max. *They're Playing Our Song: Conversations with America's Classic Songwriters*, revised edition. Westport, CT: Easton Studio Press, 2008.

Williams, Mary E., ed. *Readings on* West Side Story. San Diego: Greenhaven Press, 2001.

Winters, David. *Tough Guys Do Dance*. Pensacola, FL: Indigo River Publishing, 2018.

Zadan, Craig. *Sondheim & Co*. 2nd Edition. New York: Harper & Row, 1986.

PERIODICALS, DOCUMENTARIES, AND MISCELLANEOUS

Hollywood Reporter

Look Up and Live. CBS Television, 1958.

Los Angeles Times

New Republic

New Yorker

New York Post

New York Times

Newsweek

Saturday Review

Show

Time

Variety

Washington Post

West Side Memories. Directed by Michael Arick. Documentary, 2003.

West Side Stories: The Making of a Classic. BBC documentary, 2016.

West Side Stories: The Making of West Side Story. Directed by Peter Fitzgerald. Unreleased documentary, 1995.

ACKNOWLEDGMENTS

West Side Story, as a film and as a show, is a work of nearly unrelenting intensity. It's fitting, then, that the process of researching and writing a book about it has been quite intense in its own right. Surely it hasn't been as physically strenuous as, say, being called on to execute Jerome Robbins choreography (especially in a parking garage), yet the process has been, in a good way, taxing. Fortunately, there was always the focus and the inspiration provided by the work itself and by the people whose help and kindness made this book possible. That brings up two prominent factors I encountered while doing my work. Both were already known to me yet became more prominent as the work continued.

The first of these factors is the remarkable esteem with which people continue to hold the film *West Side Story*. The enthusiasm with which it was greeted in 1961 has not, for millions, dimmed by so much as a particle. It may not be the aim of this book to explore all the reasons why it affects so many so deeply; that would require many more pages of text and, really, a huge number of individual case histories. Still, it is my hope that the people who care so greatly about *West Side Story* will find that this book has perhaps answered a few questions, clarified a few points, and both reflected and respected their passion.

The other factor that became clearer to me also concerns a kind of passion. It is, in this case, the extraordinary amount of devotion, artistry, and hard work that went into creating this film. Time after time, while researching this film's creative evolution, I was struck by the commitment and skill with which everyone approached it. No one wanted to phone it in—which is why, of course, it went so wildly over schedule and budget, and why its production began with two directors and concluded with one. It is thus no wonder that the work has continued to have such resonance for so many of its participants, who knew then and know (even more so) now that being involved with this project was a once-in-a-lifetime experience. How many other films, after all, have earned an entire book composed entirely of the memories and reflections of the people who performed in it? (It's called *Our Story*, and it is listed in the Bibliography.) Nearly everyone associated with the film has been called on, repeatedly, to share their thoughts and recollections, and the abundance with which they have done so is testament to their professional dedication and also, again, to the personal impact that so many experienced in connection with this film. My gratitude and appreciation must thus be twofold: one for the generosity with which people have recalled their association with the film, and—even more so—for the artistry of the work they did to make it so special in the first place. I would like to give special thanks to Walter Mirisch, and also to Larry Mirisch, for verifying and clarifying a number of important points related to the complicated process involved in bringing this film to the screen. Sincere gratitude as well to Diane Baker, who figured prominently in the casting process, and to Carole d'Andrea, who had the rare distinction of creating a role in the original show and then being called upon to play it again in the film.

West Side Story has long had a happy association with Turner Classic Movies, both in airings, often as an "Essential," and through its spotlighting in such special screenings as the TCM Classic Film Festival. TCM continues to be an unparalleled treasure for a huge international audience, and it is both a pleasure and an honor to be continuing, through this book, my own happy association with the network. Naturally, it takes a large number of intrepid and talented people to keep such a terrific and successful enterprise running for well over a quarter-century. My thanks, then, to the entire TCM family and, especially, to Heather Margolis, Genevieve McGillicuddy, Jennifer Dorian, and John Malahy.

In researching this film, as researching any major film, libraries and archives are essential resources. The Margaret Herrick Library at the Academy of Motion Pictures Arts and Sciences has long been a prime go-to place for historians, and their resources remain astounding. So, for that matter, are the holdings of the Library of Congress and the New York Library for the Performing Arts at Lincoln Center, with its indispensable Jerome Robbins Dance Division. My special thanks, at the Lincoln Center Library, to Kevin Winkler. For the specific purposes of *West Side Story*, the Cinematic Arts Library at the University of Southern California was a godsend. (If Robert Wise did not save absolutely everything, he came darned close.) That there are so many precious documents and artifacts housed at USC would be boon enough. However, they reside there under the watchful and informed eye of Ned Comstock, who knows this collection as well as Jerome Robbins knew *West Side Story*. Ned has long been the film historian's best and most essential friend, with knowledge, helpfulness, enthusiasm, and sheer kindness that make him one in far more than a million. My thanks also to Photofest and Howard Mandelbaum and to Manoah Bowman for their help and generosity.

The words "personal" and "professional" are obviously quite separate, yet they can often overlap during the course of a project such as this. So many professional associates are treasured friends, and so many personal friends and family members have given me wise professional guidance that has been greatly helpful and deeply appreciated. I must first thank Jeffrey Smith, whose insight, guidance, support, interest, care, and feeding were all essential in making this book happen. Cynthia Robertson's wisdom, enthusiasm, and sharp eyes have been more helpful, and more appreciated, than words can express. As for Jane Klain, who knows nearly everything and everybody, I feel safe in terming her "a joy forever." My great appreciation and affection must also go to a quartet of friends who are major professionals in their respective fields: my darling Marilee Bradford, Jon Burlingame, David Pierce, and Christopher Diehl. There are many friends, family, and colleagues who I must thank, most joyfully. In New York, I salute, among many others: Mary and Edward Maguire, John and Roseann Forde, the Rev. Amy Gregory and Bill Phillips, Moshe Bloxenheim, Marc Miller, Edward Walters, Adele Greene, Mark Milano, Lawrence Maslon, Karen Hartman, Michael Portantiere, Ronni Krasnow, Eric Spilker, Mark Heller, Larry Gallagher, Patty Maxwell and Kevin Kostyn, Bob Gutowski, Connie Coddington, Rick Scheckman, and Vince Giordano. In Connecticut, Lou and Sue Sabini, Rick Rodgers, and Chip Reed and Christopher Fray. In Louisiana, my family and many, many friends. In particular, my wonderful sister, Rev. Peggy Foreman; nephew and great-nephews Jared, Luke, Andrew, Nathan, and Zachary Foreman; Keith Matherne, Keith Caillouet, Rev. Ned Pitre, Murray Dennis, Lorna Gianelloni, Darren Guin, and my many friends, relatives, and classmates. Elsewhere in the United States: Karen Latham Everson, William Grant and Patrick Lacey, Christopher Connelly and James Goodwynne, Joe, Katie, and Dr. Melanie Mitchell; Mark A. Vieira, Lee Tsiantis, Dennis Millay, David Thibodeaux, John

Reentz, Richard Glazier, Beverly Burt and her family, Gerry Orlando, David Litofsky, Janine Lieberman, Marcus Galante, Melissa Snyder, and Lisa Poteet. A special and deeply-felt thank you, also, to my international friends: Paul Brennan (Australia), Jonas Norden (Sweden), Aureo Chiesse Brandão (Brazil), and Andrew Henderson (Scotland). In my current home state of New Jersey, so many friends and neighbors have been such bright beacons of light and kindness that I hope that they don't mind my referring to them as my own personal Jets and Sharks. (In the most positive sense, of course.) They include, among many others, Amy, Paul and Eliza Bent; Hal Robertson, Joann Carney, Karen Van Hoy, Lawrence and Rosalind Bulk, and Marsha Bancroft. Also, all the grand people at Beverly Methodist Church and Meals of Love, including the lovely and gifted folks who make my work as music director so rewarding. To all of these people, and to those I didn't call out by name: please know that this book exists because of your care, friendship, interest, and support.

The word "support" also applies to all the people who have done so much to make this book a physical reality. I will start off by stating a simple, inarguable fact: without my editor, Cindy Sipala, there would be no book. As with our previous work together, *Must-See Musicals*, she has given me all the guidance I've asked for, all the freedom to create that I've desired, and the exact kind of supervision an author requires. I must also give my sincere thanks to Aaron Spiegeland at

Parham Santana; Running Press's publisher, Kristin Kiser; designer Celeste Joyce; and publicist Seta Zink.

It is with great reluctance that I must now use the word "finally." During the time I spent working on this book, I lost several close friends—all of them far too soon and with terrible suddenness. They supported my work in marvelous and stirring ways, and they are irreplaceable. Many people who love musical film are familiar with the name Ron Hutchinson, and for good reason. In his work with the Vitaphone Project, Ron was responsible for the restoration of countless musical films, both shorts and features. He was a wonder, a person of such energy and enthusiasm that it's still a head-scratcher to contemplate that he's left us. The comfort, such as it is, comes in the vastness of his legacy. Spencer Gauthreaux was my cousin, my confidante, and one of the funniest and dearest and warmest people I've ever had the privilege to know. He was and is, utterly and absolutely, one of a kind. As for Joe Gallagher, he was the best kind of best friend: wise beyond measure, talented beyond imagining, an eternal source of counsel and kindness, and a companion and cohort like no other. A world without Joe will remain a dimmer and less generous place indeed. These three great men, like all the people I've named (and not named) here, have impacted my work and my life in ways too vast to contemplate. A committee should be organized to honor each and every one of them. Thank you again, and God bless us all.

INDEX